SHARE JESUS WITHOUT FEAR

WILLIAM FAY & RALPH HODGE

LifeWay Press®

Nashville, Tennessee

© 1997 LifeWay Press®

Revised 2008

Third printing 2011

No part of this book may be reproduced or transmitted in any form or by any means, electronic or mechanical, including photocopying and recording, or by any information storage or retrieval system, except as may be expressly permitted in writing by the publisher. Requests for permission should be addressed in writing to LifeWay Press®; One LifeWay Plaza; Nashville, TN 37234-0175.

ISBN 978-1-4158-6534-7

Item 005146133

Dewey decimal classification: 269.2

Subject heading: EVANGELISM

Unless otherwise indicated, Scripture quotations are taken from the Holman Christian Standard Bible®, copyright © 1999, 2000, 2002, 2003 by Holman Bible Publishers. Used by permission. Scripture quotations marked NIV are taken from the Holy Bible, New International Version, copyright © 1973, 1978, 1984 by International Bible Society.

To order additional copies of this resource, write to LifeWay Church Resources Customer Service; One LifeWay Plaza; Nashville, TN 37234-0113; fax order to (615) 251-5933; e-mail *orderentry@lifeway.com;* phone toll free (800) 458-2772; order online at *www.lifeway.com;* or visit the LifeWay Christian Store serving you.

Printed in the United States of America

Leadership and Adult Publishing

LifeWay Church Resources

One LifeWay Plaza

Nashville, TN 37234-0175

CONTENTS

PREFACE

I am so glad you have chosen to study *Share Jesus Without Fear*. Most faithful Christians want to share their faith. Many have tried, received a negative reaction, felt rejected, and thought they had failed. As a result, they do not witness anymore and now feel guilty. Other Christians simply don't know how to share their faith. I can make you a promise that God fulfills every time *Share Jesus Without Fear* is taught: you will realize that you absolutely cannot fail when you share your faith! Because the three-step process presented in this study is so simple, you may wonder why you have not been taught this approach before.

Let me introduce myself. I am evangelist William Fay, a sinner saved by grace. For 40 years of my life, I was antagonistic to the gospel. Many Christians tried to share their faith with me, and I insulted, persecuted, or antagonized them. However, if they walked away from me believing they had failed, they believed a lie. I never forgot any of the words, the faces, or the persons who came into my life in obedience to Jesus Christ.

I have had the privilege of sharing my faith on a one-to-one basis many thousands of times. But as an evangelist, I am certain that I have never led one person to Jesus Christ. However, I have been around many times when the Holy Spirit has done it. Success is sharing your faith—living your life for Jesus Christ. It has nothing to do with bringing anyone to the Lord. We are not responsible for causing a conversion in anyone's life. In fact, if you and I caused the conversion, that person isn't saved! Conversion is the work of the Holy Spirit.

As you have heard many times, the Great Commission says, "Go!" It is not an option to consider but a command that God says must be obeyed. The Bible tells us that if we don't do what is good, it is sin: "For the person who knows to do good and doesn't do it, it is a sin" (Jas. 4:17). If you have not been active in sharing your faith, you have committed the sin of silence. I am deeply concerned for all God's people who are disobedient in this area of life. They will be humbled for disobedience in not keeping God's command.

In many years of speaking in churches, I have rarely found that more than 10 percent of any church congregation, regardless of the denomination, had shared their faith in the past year. How can faithful church members say they experience a meaningful worship time on Sunday but remain silent on Monday?

Tens of thousands of people have found the method presented in this book simple to use because you don't have to memorize a presentation and because you totally depend on the Holy Spirit, using the Word of God. No one will be able to argue with you. You will use nonthreatening questions to discover how God is working in someone's life. And you will watch Philemon 6 come alive in your life: "I pray that you may be active in sharing your faith, so that you will have a full understanding of every good thing we have in Christ" (NIV).

Can you imagine the joy of knowing that you cannot fail when you choose obedience to Jesus Christ by sharing your faith? You will experience God's power working through you as you see Him change lives for all eternity through your witness. You will observe the power of God's Word firsthand as you turn the pages of Scripture and see the Holy Spirit transform lives before your eyes.

If you apply what you learn in this study, the lives of many individuals who cross your path will be changed. Of equal importance, your life will be changed forever.

In His grip and grace,
Evangelist William Fay

The illustration of the farmer (week 1), the psychiatrist (week 1), and the choking victim (week 3) are personal experiences of Ralph Hodge. All other personal encounters and illustrations are those of William Fay.

WEEK 1

DEVELOPING A HEART
TO SHARE JESUS

Have you ever had an opportunity to share your faith but didn't?

Opening (8 minutes)

- Distribute *Share Jesus Without Fear* workbooks to participants.
- Turn to page 7 and ask group members to share their responses to this question: *Have you ever had an opportunity to share your faith but didn't?* Ask them to share some reasons they did not.

DVD (10:30 minutes)

- View the first DVD segment, "Introductory Overview and the Sin of Silence: Part 1." When the screen instructs you, stop.
  1. Peter denied Jesus three times.
  2. We deny Jesus Christ by our silence.

Facilitator-Led Conversation (5 minutes)

- In your own words, what is the sin of silence?
- Discuss the following.
  1. Peter denied Jesus three times. We deny Him by our silence.
  2. Why do we commit the sin of silence?

DVD (7:30 minutes)

- View the second DVD segment, "The Sin of Silence: Part 2." When the screen instructs you, stop.
  1. The sin of silence affects your personal life.
  2. The sin of silence affects our churches.

Facilitator-Led Conversation (5 minutes)

- Would you admit that you have been guilty of the sin of silence? Note: Someone may ask, "Where does it say in the Bible that this is a sin?" Jesus' command in Matthew 28:19 is to "go and make disciples" (NIV). Failure to go is rebellion against God.

- Before you return to the DVD, ask: *What are some reasons you are afraid to share your faith?* List fears mentioned in the margin.

DVD (7:30 minutes)

- View the third DVD segment, "The Sin of Silence: Part 3." When the screen instructs you, stop.

Facilitator-Led Conversation (10 minutes)

- Some fears that prevent people from sharing their faith:
  1. Fear of rejection
  2. I don't know enough.
  3. What if people get offended?
  4. I'm uncomfortable sharing at work.
  5. I'm afraid my life isn't what it ought to be.
  6. What if I am ridiculed and persecuted for sharing?
  7. I'm not good at evangelism.

- Discuss the fears mentioned by the group and in the DVD segment.
- How do we overcome these fears?
- Discuss the following quotation by Bill Fay: "Success in witnessing is living the Christian life daily, sharing the gospel, and trusting God for the results. Success is not bringing someone to Christ."
- Before this study did you think success in witnessing was winning someone to Christ?
- What does it mean to trust God for the results?
- What has God taught you during this session?

Closing (1 minute)

- Complete week 1 in the workbook.
- Prayer.

It is possible to lead others to faith

in Christ without being out of character

or offensive. God has called every Christian to be a witness—

- by the way we live;

- by our attitude toward others;

- by the choices we make;

- by our commitment to live for Jesus at any cost.

God has also called every Christian to witness by personally showing lost people how they can be spiritually reborn.

Share Jesus Without Fear will show you how to be successful when witnessing to those who are spiritually lost. It will change your life. You will learn that success is more than leading someone to Christ. Success is living the Christian life daily, sharing the gospel, and trusting God for the results.

Success is living the Christian life daily, sharing the gospel, and trusting God for the results.

This study will give you a series of questions you can ask lost people to discover their receptivity to the love of Jesus. These questions can help you sense how God is working in lost people's lives and how open they are to hearing God's invitation. Their answers will lead to a change that can affect their lives forever. The Bible will provide guidance. And if lost people are ready to hear, God's power will penetrate the lack of knowledge, doubts, and objections that have been barriers in their lives.

The Bible does not present witnessing as an extra activity done only by a few special people. Witnessing as a Christian is normal. It is to be part of each Christian's daily life whenever opportunities occur. God is at work all around you creating opportunities for you to share the gospel. Creating witnessing opportunities is His work. Our part is to be obedient, to act on these moments that God is creating.

What is your greatest fear about witnessing?

One study revealed that most of us rarely, if ever, witness to the lost because of our struggle with four major fears (see day 5 for more on these fears):
- Fear of being rejected
- Fear of not knowing enough
- Fear of offending a friend or relative
- Fear of being ridiculed or persecuted

God provides the opportunity to witness, and He promises His power to help us. Yet we simply say no. Because of fear, our no is accompanied by much defense and justification; but to say no to God for any reason is sin. The first step for each of us to become a witnessing Christian is a change in our heart. We must choose obedience to God: "Set apart the Messiah as Lord in your hearts, and always be ready to give a defense to anyone who asks you for a reason for the hope that is in you. However, do this with gentleness and respect" (1 Pet. 3:15-16).

Debate has flourished about which of the wounds inflicted on Jesus actually caused His death. Among the many wounds He received were lacerations, punctures, abrasions, and contusions. In a sense we can say that none of these killed Jesus. The wound that killed Him was silence. No one spoke up for Him. One of the most painful incidents in Jesus' life was Peter's denial of Him the night before His crucifixion. Three times Peter was asked whether he was Jesus' follower, and three times he said no. I've said in my own heart and I've heard many others say, "I would never have denied Him like that."

Identify a time when you had an opportunity to share your faith but didn't.

List some of the reasons you did not witness.

Most of us can recall times when we chose to be silent when we could have witnessed. When we are silent, we, like Peter, deny Jesus. Peter probably thought it only made sense not to put himself in danger. Many of us have also decided that it is only reasonable not to risk being rejected, embarrassed, or persecuted. We choose to be silent.

Another form of the sin of silence is to witness just enough to ease our conscience or establish our Christian image. We tell people we love the Lord. We eagerly tell people we'll pray for them. We may even have a Christian bumper sticker. We must admit, though, that we don't share enough information with lost people to allow the Holy Spirit to change their hearts. We fail to tell our friends they can be called out of darkness and into His wonderful light (see 1 Pet. 2:9). If we don't share our faith, our friends may never understand the gospel and may never have an opportunity to be led by the Holy Spirit to believe.

If we don't share our faith, our friends may never understand the gospel and may never have an opportunity to be led by the Holy Spirit to believe.

A boy was picking up starfish from a beach and throwing them one at a time back into the ocean. A man said, "Son, look down that way." As far as the boy could see, the shore was covered with starfish. "Now look up that way." As far as he could see, the shore was covered with starfish. "Son," the man said, "you can't expect to throw all of those back. No matter how many you throw back, there will still be more left on shore." Picking up a starfish, the boy threw it back into the sea and said, "Well, I sure made a difference for that one."

Like that single starfish, one person's world can change every time you share the gospel. Although it is an incredible thought, it is possible that God, working through you, could change the course of history. If you need proof of this truth, look in the mirror; when you heard the gospel, your life changed forever. A lost friend's life depends on knowing the truth.

We must never lose sight of the destiny of people who do not choose to live for Christ. Many people who know what the Bible teaches about eternal life attempt to find middle ground. I once lived what I now call the lie of the middle. Somehow I believed I wasn't that bad, that I was in the "middle" and therefore deserved to go to heaven. Now I know that was a lie.

What do you think is wrong with living in the middle?

Trying to live in the middle is living a lie. The truth is, either you follow God, or you follow Satan. Either you are in a relationship with Christ, or you're not. Either you're born again, or you're not. You are either God's child or God's enemy. Either you are storing up wrath, or you are storing up mercy. You are either heaven bound or hell bound. No one is in the middle. No one is almost there. Those who have chosen to reject Christ are condemned.

We must quit believing the lie that claims God will look the other way when our family and friends who have no relationship with Christ stand before Him. We must refuse to believe that God will allow our unbelieving friends to bypass hell and join us in heaven.

There are two kinds of people in our churches:

1. Those who talk about the lost
2. Those who talk to the lost

Check the phrase that most accurately describes you.
- ❑ **I talk about the lost.**
- ❑ **I talk to the lost.**

The great concern as you hear God speak now is not which of these two kinds of people you are. The great concern is which you will choose to become after learning this simple approach to sharing Jesus.

During the first week of this study, you will encounter the sin of silence. You will also learn how to face and overcome your fears, understanding that obedience to Christ is possible because of His presence, power, and joy in you. You will gain the confidence and the desire to overcome any fear. In week 2 you will learn how you can use simple questions effectively to lead a person to faith in Christ. In week 3 you will learn how to let the Bible provide answers, and you will discover the importance of silence and prayer in listening as the Holy Spirit speaks. You will learn five closing questions that recap the key verses and lead lost people to ask Christ to become part of their lives.

Remember, you can't fail if you're faithful. As God works in the life of an unbeliever, you will find yourself guiding that person to Christ and being a part of His work. Always remember that the Bible will provide the answers. The Holy Spirit will provide the power.

PASSION

It was early spring, and the hope of the new season was reflected in the worship service I was attending. But hope was not to be found everywhere in the community. During the service the pastor read a letter he had received from a woman who lived near the church. She was asking for prayer and help for her family. Recently, her husband had become involved in drugs and, as a result, was about to go to prison. Making matters worse, the family had been contacted by a social agency that was to assume custody of their children. The woman was desperate. The pastor went to the address on the letter and found the family at home. He led the husband and the wife to surrender their hearts to faith in Christ as Savior and Lord.

Later, while the man and his wife stood in the baptistry during a worship service, the pastor mentioned the letter that led him to this couple. He asked the woman, "How did you happen to write our church?" She responded, "I did not just write your church. I wrote all the churches in the community. You were the only one who answered."

Would your church have responded the way this one did?
❑ Yes   ❑ No

Would you?
❑ Yes   ❑ No

God wants every Christian to have a heart for lost people. Yet passion for witnessing to non-Christians is far more than a zeal for witnessing. It is zeal based on a purpose. It is love for God and for people that drives us to witness. The love that led this pastor to respond is nurtured by a desire to love people and to give them hope that is found only in a relationship with Jesus.

Sometimes a simple question or statement about your own faith in Jesus provides a grip on a loose thread in a lost person's heart. A caring person can mend a heart of brokenness, bring hope to a heart of hopelessness, and bring salvation to a heart that is lost without Jesus.

Several years ago I began asking Christians to think about how many times they heard the gospel before they came to a point of trusting in Jesus as Savior. I found that Christians heard the gospel an average of 7.6 times before surrendering to Christ after the seventh time. Therefore, on average the lost person received Jesus just after the seventh touch. You may not know whether the person standing beside you has ever been touched, has been touched once, or has been touched 6 times. But this doesn't matter, because success is found in obedience.

Success is found in obedience.

Have you ever witnessed to someone who did not then accept Christ? ❑ **Yes** ❑ **No**

How did you feel and respond?

Remember, when your witness does not result in the immediate surrender of a person's life to Christ, you are likely to be one of several touches of God in the lost person's life. Being witnessed to and hearing a sermon are just two of the many ways God may touch the person's life. For the lost persons in your life, you may be the key that opens their heart to God, or you may represent one of 7 or 8 knocks on his or her heart's door. You may be the first touch. You may be number 7 or 10 or 30.

A passion for witnessing is more like love than determination. Jesus had a passion that drove Him to make the way of salvation known in spite of rejection, suffering, and ultimately the cross. He proclaimed His desire for us to share His heart for lost people when He said, "As the Father has sent Me, I also send you" (John 20:21).

A great deal is written today about the need for churches to be driven by appropriate purpose and vision. The Book of Acts could not be clearer as it presents the purpose and passion driving the church: to share with the world what Jesus came to do. Jesus was driven by His mission to bridge the dark, wide abyss that separates a person from being reconciled to God. When confronted by the Sadducees for sharing the gospel, Peter and John answered, "We are unable to stop speaking about what we have seen and heard" (Acts 4:20).

The apostle Paul described his passion for reaching lost people in 1 Corinthians 9:19-23. He was willing to make personal sacrifices and become "a slave to all" in order to share his love for Christ and to witness to the lost. This does not mean that he compromised truth and right. A person can adapt to individual needs without compromising doctrinally and biblically. Paul kept the purpose before him: "I have become all things to all people, so that I may by all means save some" (1 Cor. 9:22).

Look deeply into your heart. Because the Holy Spirit lives within you, you have always had a desire to share Jesus with others. Take time to confess that to God. Tell Him that you want to be a part of His plan, to be a willing servant, to experience God in deeper ways as He works through your life.

Most Christians have longed for a more meaningful, deeper relationship with God. Spiritual growth comes as you join God in doing your part to fulfill His purposes. Courage to witness will follow your deepening walk with God. As you trust Him with your confession of sin and failures, your desire to trust and please Him will unleash His power in you as a witness.

The passion you should have for reaching lost people is not related to fanaticism or high-pressure sales. Obey Paul's instruction: "Your speech should always be gracious" (Col. 4:6). In Romans 12:11 Paul tells us, "Never be lacking in zeal, but keep your spiritual fervor, serving the Lord" (NIV). Zeal, or passion, is clearly a virtue to nurture. But remember the counsel of Solomon: "Even zeal is not good without knowledge" (Prov. 19:2). Your passion must be grounded in obedience to God's purpose.

Think about the persons God worked through to bring you to trust Jesus as Savior and Lord. Write their names.

What did they share with you?

Where would you be without those who loved both God and you enough to obey His command to witness?

What would your life be like without Jesus?

There is an important difference between loving to reach lost people and loving lost people. If you love only the activity without learning to love people as Jesus did, you will sooner or later lose interest and move on to another activity.

The Bible allows us to observe Jesus facing many demands but staying focused on His passion. In Capernaum "all those who had anyone sick with various diseases brought them to Him. As He laid His hands on each one of them, He would heal them" (Luke 4:40). The people wanted Him to continue this healing work. But Jesus refused to stay, saying, "I must proclaim the good news about the kingdom of God to the other towns also, because I was sent for this purpose" (Luke 4:43). He never lost view of His main purpose. His main purpose was to proclaim how lost people are saved. Even the wonderful healing of the sick was secondary to the work of keeping lost people from dying without knowing the way to eternal life.

Why should we witness? Jesus commanded us. The primary mission of the church is to establish a way for every lost person to hear the news of salvation through faith in Jesus Christ. The greatest way to honor someone is to introduce him or her to Jesus Christ. There are clear reasons you must accept your responsibility to share Jesus.

"All authority has been given to Me in heaven and on earth. Go, therefore, and make disciples of all nations, baptizing them in the name of the Father and of the Son and of the Holy Spirit, teaching them to observe everything I have commanded you. And remember, I am with you always, to the end of the age."
MATTHEW 28:18-20

The Great Commission is directed to every Christian. Witnessing is not optional for a Christian who wants to be obedient and faithful to all God asks. The Great Commission is not an option to be considered but a command to be obeyed.

The accurate translation of *go* in Matthew 28:19 is *as you are going.* As you are going, make disciples. As you are going, baptize converts in the name of the Father and of the Son and of the Holy Spirit. As you are going, teach them to obey everything I have commanded you. Jesus promised that, as you witness, He will be with you. Witnessing is to become part of your response whenever an opportunity comes or can be initiated. A deepening relationship with Jesus results in a growing desire to tell others about Him. As you live your life in a closer relationship with Jesus, you will develop a greater awareness of opportunities to witness. Witnessing seldom requires extra time in your busy schedule, just greater awareness.

Jesus' command for us to go to lost people provides instructions to do three major tasks:

1. Be sensitive to the needs of lost people.
2. In obedience share your faith in Jesus.
3. Help them find a church where they can grow spiritually.

The word *compulsion* may best describe the passion that drives a person to witness. For some Christians, knowing that people are lost presents a decision as to whether they will attempt to witness. Christians with a passion for sharing Jesus, however, don't decide each time they have an opportunity. The decision has already been made conclusively. The decision is not "Should I attempt to approach or respond to this lost person?" but "How am I going to approach or respond to this lost person?"

Review on page 12 the reasons you have put off sharing your faith. Pray, confessing that no reason is good enough to fail to share the good news of Jesus. Ask God to help you become an obedient witness through this study.

2 PRAYER

Nothing is more important in developing a heart for witnessing than prayer. Prayer makes the difference. The Holy Spirit works, the barriers fall, and the gentle hand of God guides you to opportunities for sharing and obedience.

Witnessing does not require intense training or the accumulation of extensive theological learning. It is supernatural work.

Witnessing does not require intense training or the accumulation of extensive theological learning. It is supernatural work. Prayer connects you with the supernatural power of God. With this power your personal witness becomes more art than science. For some reason, many people believe it is much more difficult to become a Christian than it actually is. You need to remember how little you knew when you first believed.

At times a witness overestimates the need for a particular witnessing approach. A professional method is not required. The heart of the witness has far more impact than any approach! As you will see in weeks 2 and 3, preparation is extremely important. But what could prepare the heart of a successful witness more than the spiritual power brought by prayer?

The heart of the witness has far more impact than any approach!

Consistent prayer prepares your heart for any encounter. Once at the conclusion of a worship service, I gave an invitation for people to come forward to pray for lost loved ones. While many were in small groups weeping and praying, I felt the Holy Spirit urging me to the church foyer. There I noticed a man, Phil, standing alone. When

I asked him whether he regularly attended church, he responded, "No." I said to him, "Do you know the Lord?" He replied, "Known Him all my life."

Although Phil claimed to have known the Lord all his life, he could not look me in the eye and tell me that he was born again. When I asked him about this, he said that he wasn't saved but that he wanted to be. "Who brought you this morning?" I asked. He told me that he had come with his brother and sister-in-law. When we had found our way back to the altar, I noticed his sister-in-law in a group praying. As I approached, I heard her praying for her brother-in-law's salvation.

Phil's life was transformed that morning by the power of God. Moreover, a praying sister-in-law was transformed as she experienced the power of God. The Bible tells us, "The intense prayer of the righteous is very powerful" (Jas. 5:16).

Prayer is the primary way you develop a close relationship with God. In prayer you become plugged into the power of God to develop a godly heart. Prayer develops a Christian's inner life. Apart from a prayer relationship with God, you are mostly talking about Him rather than talking with Him. The close relationship a person has with God through prayer remains the key to developing a heart of compassion. Simply put, you will find the heart of God in prayer—and the discovery will change your life.

Prayer deepens your relationship with Jesus. Balancing inner spiritual growth and other activities—teaching, caring for preschoolers, facilitating a discipleship group, serving on an outreach or ministry committee—depends on a prayer relationship with God. Christians who witness to unbelievers will find themselves in a spiritual struggle if they do not maintain a regular prayer routine. You can become so busy in spiritual activity that you fail to develop your own inner spiritual relationship with God.

List the Christian activities you are involved in.

How do you balance these activities and prayer?

One church dedicated each week's prayer meeting to pray for the world of lost people. After several weeks of these meetings, one member stood and said he was going to pray a different prayer. "We don't need to pray for the lost people of the world. God knows who they are and where they are," he said. He went on to say that praying for the lost is not enough. It doesn't do any good to pray for the lost if that's all we do. He said he was going to begin to pray as Jesus asked him to pray—for more workers in the field.

It is important to pray for lost people by name. Be careful, however, that you don't just pray for lost people. God needs people who will take the good news to the lost. Pray for God to touch your own heart. Ask Him to burden you for the harvest.

While I was serving as a pastor in a farming community, God gave me an experience that changed my prayer life forever. Answering my telephone one afternoon, I recognized the desperate and strained voice of a farmer who had seen dark clouds moving toward his farm. Because the weather forecasters hadn't predicted rain, he had acres of newly cut hay still lying in the fields waiting to be taken to the barns. A farmer fears an unexpected storm because the rain will cause his hay to rot and become useless.

The farmer told me his son was in a truck heading for town to pick up migrant workers and other temporary laborers who gathered there each morning. But because it was afternoon, he feared that the workers had already given up on work for the day and gone home. I will never forget the desperation in this faithful Christian farmer's voice. He asked me, "Please pray that there will be workers at the corner and enough to help me get my hay up before it rains."

The prayer request wasn't for the hay in his fields. The hay wasn't going anywhere. He didn't appeal for prayer so that the rain wouldn't come. His hope was to find enough workers he could depend on to do what needed to be done.

While praying for the lost, I have often heard that farmer's voice appealing to God for enough workers. At the same time, I also hear Jesus' voice as He asks us to pray for people willing to go to the lost and tell them how to be saved: "The harvest is abundant, but the workers are few. Therefore, pray to the Lord of the harvest to send out workers into His harvest" (Matt. 9:37-38).

> "The harvest is abundant, but the workers are few. Therefore, pray to the Lord of the harvest to send out workers into His harvest."
>
> MATTHEW 9:37-38

Evaluate your prayer life. Check the things you most commonly pray about.
- ❑ **Your physical and financial needs**
- ❑ **Your family, friends, and church**
- ❑ **Your spiritual needs**
- ❑ **Witnessing opportunities**
- ❑ **Salvation for the lost**
- ❑ **Workers in the harvest of lost people**

Describe specific ways your prayer life needs to change if you are to be faithful in praying for the needs of the lost. Ask God to touch your heart and to burden you for the harvest.

Paul encouraged Philemon: "I pray that you may be active in sharing your faith, so that you will have a full understanding of every good thing we have in Christ" (Philem. 6, NIV). Paul knew that Philemon would grow in his relationship with Christ as he shared his faith with unbelievers. Witnessing always deepens your personal faith. God reaches lost persons through your obedience, but He also transforms your life and deepens your relationship with Him.

DAY 3 PARTNERSHIP

Sharing Jesus is not a solo sport; it is partnership—with Christ. The essential ingredients for a true partnership are trust and commitment. You must witness with trust in the power of God. You must also be committed to do your part. Many Christians tend to be spectators who admire the efforts of those who proclaim the gospel and witness. Yet commitment is more than admiration:

- It means you have to offer your life in deep involvement in Christ's life—in His teachings, in His moral standards, in His death and resurrection, in everything He's said and done.
- It means you have to share in deep involvement in the lives of people—not standing by as a spectator watching to see how it goes but to be there where it's happening.[1]

From the earliest times God has promised that living our lives for Him would be a partnership.

From the earliest times God has promised that living our lives for Him would be a partnership. God told Joshua, "I will be with you, just as I was with Moses. I will not leave you or forsake you" (Josh. 1:5). He went on to assure Joshua, "Haven't I commanded you: be strong and courageous? Do not be afraid or discouraged, for the LORD your God is with you wherever you go" (Josh. 1:9). Witnessing to a lost person is no smaller a challenge than God gave Joshua. There is no greater work for Christians than to help lost people know the truth of Jesus dying on the cross for their sins.

Jesus has promised us the presence and partnership of His Spirit, who is our paraclete. Paraclete is a Greek word that means one who is a helper, one who will never leave you. The Holy Spirit will be present to fulfill God's promises and to give you His power for doing the things He asks. Jesus said, "It is for your benefit that I go away, because if I don't go away the Counselor [Paraclete] will not come to you. … When He comes, He will convict the world about sin, righteousness, and judgment" (John 16:7-8).

Because you are God's partner, He has planned particular things for you to accomplish with Him. You cannot expect someone else to do the things God has asked of you just because he or she seems more capable. God brought Aaron into partnership with Moses, but Moses was not relieved of the responsibility to do what God had asked him to do. Partners depend on each other to be where they're expected to be and to do what they're expected to do. A worthwhile partnership requires consistency and courage, responsibility and dependability. A worthwhile partnership has—

- a worthy purpose that cannot be accomplished without the help of the other partner;
- an agreed-on strategy for the task.

The relationship between God and His witness is a thread running throughout the Bible.

The relationship between God and His witness is a thread running throughout the Bible. God found Gideon under an oak tree and called him to deliver Israel from Midian (see Judg. 6:11-14). God listened as Gideon rehearsed reasons he was not the person to do it. God had certainly heard these kinds of objections before. Gideon argued, "Please, Lord, how can I deliver Israel? Look, my family is the weakest in Manasseh, and I am the youngest in my father's house" (Judg. 6:15). Gideon sought various signs that God would provide the resources and power for him to complete the task. Yet it was Gideon, not God, being tested.

An army of 32,000 amassed behind Gideon, who was now ready to go forward leading a huge army with the promise of God's presence. But before he would confront the enemy, his army would be reduced to 300 (see Judg. 7:1-8). With nothing more than faith in God and partnership with Him, Gideon was to accomplish God's mission.

God asked Moses to go to Pharaoh and bring the Israelites out of Egypt. Moses would take the lead in making God's message known (see Ex. 3:10). His reaction to the call was to give reasons he shouldn't go to tell Pharaoh God's message. These same reasons echo into our own time as many Christians speak these same protests. Moses' excuses for not wanting to go to Pharaoh with God's message were really just covers for the real reason, which he finally admitted.

Read the following Scriptures and record Moses' objections for going to Pharaoh. Also record a modern-day version of Moses' excuse that believers might use to avoid witnessing to the lost.

Read Exodus 3:11-12.

Moses' excuse:	**Today's excuse:**
Wrong guy	

Read Exodus 3:13-17.

Moses' excuse:	**Today's excuse:**
I don't know enough	*Need a prof'l.*

Read Exodus 4:1-9.

Moses' excuse:	**Today's excuse:**
They won't believe me! [God's power offered]	

Read Exodus 4:10-12.

Moses' excuse:	**Today's excuse:**
Not a good speaker Not eloquent (slow of speech)	

makes God angry!

Read Exodus 4:13.

Moses' excuse:	**Today's excuse:**
Please send someone else	

First, Moses told God that he didn't have the position or stature to approach a powerful pharaoh (see Ex. 3:11-12). Today a Christian might say, "A minister would be the best person to go to my neighbor who is lost. Ministers are trained, and people respect ministers. They'll believe them."

Second, Moses told God that the people wouldn't have a way to know that he was speaking for the true God of Israel. He, like many of us today, stated that he didn't know enough about God to convince the people (see Ex. 3:13-17). Today a Christian might say, "I don't know enough about doctrine and how to explain things about God to a lost person. Somebody who is deeply spiritual and knows a lot about God should go to my lost relatives."

Third, Moses told God that the people wouldn't believe his story (see Ex. 4:1-9). Today a Christian might say, "A lost person won't see any reason in my life to believe my witness of God's saving grace and care. Somebody who has had a miracle in his life would be the best person to witness."

Fourth, Moses told God that because he wasn't a good speaker, he couldn't talk easily or say the right things (see Ex. 4:10-12). Today a Christian might say something similar: "I don't do a good job talking about spiritual things with other people. I might say the wrong things or just confuse my lost friend."

Finally, Moses expressed the heart of most Christians today when faced with God's call to witness. Moses said, "Please, Lord, send someone else" (Ex. 4:13). Although uttered hundreds of years ago, Moses' appeal to God still represents the attitudes of many Christians toward witnessing to lost people. Just as in Moses' day, we fear that our witness will bring dishonor to God and embarrassment to ourselves.

What Moses overlooked, and what many Christians today overlook, is God's promise. In Exodus 3:12 God said, "I will certainly be with you." God called Aaron, Moses' brother, to go with him and tell the people what God had said. Working together to convince one of the world's most powerful leaders, Moses and Aaron portrayed a profound and exciting partnership. The same intimate partnership that God established with Moses exists today between God and those called to share His message. He will be with you as well.

In Acts 1:8 we read Jesus' call to every Christian. It is a call to a partnership so that the story of Jesus can be told throughout the world. God has chosen to work in partnership with Christians for many crucial things. Sharing the good news is one of the highest expressions of this partnership. If things you do are to have any lasting significance, they must be done in partnership with Christ. As Jesus said in John 15:5, "You can do nothing without Me." It is equally true, as the apostle Paul declared, that "I am able to do all things through Him who strengthens me" (Phil. 4:13).

Have you ever thought about witnessing as a partnership between you and God?   ❑ **Yes**   ❑ **No**

How does it make you feel to realize that the Holy Spirit goes with you and empowers you when you witness?

DAY 4 POWER

The prescription for spiritual power is found in Acts 1:7-8: "He said to them, 'It is not for you to know times or periods that the Father has set by His own authority. But you will receive power when the Holy Spirit has come upon you, and you will be My witnesses in Jerusalem, in all Judea and Samaria, and to the ends of the earth.' "

Jesus promised the power of the Holy Spirit for a specific purpose: "You will be My witnesses" (v. 8). Do you have difficulty witnessing for Jesus? Perhaps it will be helpful to receive a prescription for easing your fear. The prescription consists of two ingredients that will help to cure your reluctance: obedience and power. When you become obedient, God will provide the power. You will find success not only in bringing someone to Christ but also in living the Christian life daily, sharing the gospel, and trusting God for the results.

> "You will receive power when the Holy Spirit
> has come upon you, and you will be My witnesses
> in Jerusalem, in all Judea and Samaria,
> and to the ends of the earth."
>
> ACTS 1:8

Are you being obedient—

to live the Christian life daily?	❑ Yes	❑ No
to share the gospel?	❑ Yes	❑ No
to trust God for the results?	❑ Yes	❑ No

In all you do, you can claim the power of a higher love because you know what Christ has done: "No one has greater love than this, that someone would lay down his life for his friends" (John 15:13). Paul wanted to know this "power of His resurrection" above all else (Phil. 3:10). This power is yours because Christ is alive in you. The power that has overcome dark death is the same power you can call on to overcome all obstacles to being a faithful witness to a lost world. God's will is for each Christian to witness; yet you must call on the same power that delivered Jesus from death to deliver you from a dependence on your own ability and skills. You must depend on the power of God. Jesus tells us of the limitless possibilities that accompany anything you do in His power and love: "The one who believes in Me will also do the works that I do. And he will do even greater works than these, because I am going to the Father. Whatever you ask in My name, I will do it so that the Father may be glorified in the Son" (John 14:12-13).

> ## "Whatever you ask in My name, I will do it so that the Father may be glorified in the Son."
>
> JOHN 14:13

Rejoice because you possess this resurrection power. You cannot fail if you are faithful to do what God has asked you to do. The Holy Spirit will be with you as you witness. You never need to approach any witnessing opportunity fearing that He is not with you. On the Day of Pentecost, the Holy Spirit, accompanied by extraordinary signs, poured Himself into believers. Since that day the emphasis has been on receiving. Witnessing to Jews in Jerusalem, Peter stated, "Repent … and be baptized, each of you, in the name of Jesus the Messiah for the forgiveness of your sins, and you will receive the gift of the Holy Spirit" (Acts 2:38).

> ## You cannot fail if you are faithful to do what God has asked you to do.

Name some ways the Holy Spirit works in a believer's attempt to witness.

The Holy Spirit makes your witnessing efforts effective. It is the Holy Spirit who convicts of sin and touches the heart. It is remarkable to see the Holy Spirit work as defensiveness changes to interest and as a hard heart softens to accept God's love. The difficult questions you fear become unimportant as the power generated by your partnership with God grows. You will sense the Holy Spirit working through you as He guides a lost person to ask the right questions, find the right answers, and make a decision. Trembling, fearful hesitancy is turned to joy as you see what God will do when an ordinary Christian becomes involved in an extraordinary service.

Have you ever experienced the Holy Spirit working through you as you witnessed? How did you know He was at work? Describe one experience.

If you have not had such an experience, pray that God will fill you with His Spirit and empower you to reach others with the gospel.

The power of God will be given according to the need. Remember that God has assigned you to witness, and He will not give you any task for which he hasn't already made provision. Generally, this is not a power that can be felt ahead of time. You must trust that God will keep His word when you need His wisdom and power.

Witnessing, like all other tasks God calls you to do, is based on your belief that your mission will be accomplished not by your own power but by God's presence providing the power (see Zech. 4:6). Jesus talked with a woman who had come to a well to quench her thirst (John 4:1-42). Once Jesus revealed Himself as the Messiah, the woman rushed to her village and invited the villagers to "come, see a man who told me everything I ever did!" However, in her next breath she said, "Could this be the Messiah?" (John 4:29). Her testimony to the village was made up of two statements. One part of her testimony revealed what she knew: "Come, see a man who told me everything I ever did!" Her next question, however, illustrates the hesitant nature of many: "Could this be the Messiah?" The sincerity of her witness experience is credible because these were the only things of which she was certain. Although she knew some things, a question remained in her experience with Jesus. Her testimony transformed these lost people, not because of any particular method but through the power of her love for the Lord and for others.

FACE YOUR FEARS WITH GOD'S POWER

According to one survey of Christians, the number one reason for not witnessing is fear of rejection. This fear is partly the fault of the words and phrases we use to enlist people to witness. We encourage people to be soul-winners or to bring people to Christ. These and a host of other phrases speak of action steps. Many Christians have misunderstood these terms to mean that we actually play a role in the transformation of a person from the darkness of sin to the light of life in Christ.

The truth is, God doesn't ask believers to cause the salvation of a person's soul. Sharing your faith doesn't mean that you actually bring someone to the Lord. God is the one who takes these actions. Remember, this is the one area of your Christian life in which you cannot fail. Even if your voice trembles, your hands shake, you stumble over words, you struggle to make your witness clear, or your timing is poor, God can use your witness. However, God cannot use your silence.

> People who did not surrender their lives
> to Christ when you witnessed to them
> did not reject you. They rejected Jesus.

People who did not surrender their lives to Christ when you witnessed to them did not reject you. They rejected Jesus. They rejected God's Word. It is never about you. If you witness to someone tomorrow who becomes a leading national evangelist, can you take credit for that? No. If someone you witness to the next day rejects Christ, is it your fault? No. In this area of your life, you can't take credit for the victories or the rejections.

> **Fill in the blanks to define what you have learned this week about success in witnessing. Success in witnessing is not bringing someone to Christ but _____ the Christian life daily, _____ the gospel, and _____ God for the results.**

Another fear that keeps many Christians silent is the fear of not knowing enough. This fear is expressed most often by people who have been Christians for several years. A research project revealed that most people who personally lead a lost person to the Lord do so in the first year or two after becoming a Christian. It may be true that the longer a person is a Christian, the more he realizes how little he knows about his faith. Believers sometimes become so conscious of the many things they need to learn that they forget how simple it is to be born again.

> **Check the types of knowledge that are required for you to be an effective witness.**
> - ❏ **Deep theological knowledge**
> - ❏ **A knowledge of your spiritual gifts**
> - ❏ **A knowledge of how someone can accept Jesus as Savior and Lord**
> - ❏ **A knowledge of the lost person's needs**

An abundance of knowledge is not required to be God's instrument in guiding a person to new life in Jesus. Although other types of knowledge can sometimes help, all you need to witness is an understanding of how someone can accept Jesus.

Another excuse for not witnessing is the fear of offending a friend or a relative. We often say that we will make any sacrifice for our friends and family. Yet when it comes to helping them make the most important life-and-death decision of their lives, we decide that witnessing is too much to ask.

A retired psychiatrist once spoke to me about witnessing to his daughter. She was his only child and had children of her own. He wept as he told me that he had required his family to attend church while she was growing up. While away at college, the daughter had become rebellious, and the tension resulted in little communication between them for several years.

He said to me, "God began to speak to me about my own spiritual emptiness. I realized that although I had worked for years to help people sort out and resolve problems in their lives, I had failed to help them discover the One who could provide the only real help. I had focused on the problems I now realized were actually by-products of the real problem that needed to be settled. I had failed to guide people to a trusting relationship with Jesus Christ. I knew I had failed my family as well." He told me he had called his daughter and asked if he could come talk with her. In her home he asked his only daughter, "Do you really have any kind of spiritual belief? Tell me who Jesus is to you." He described how God opened her heart and how they later knelt beside the kitchen table as she confessed her sins and surrendered her life to Jesus.

**Do you have family and friends who need to come
to Christ? List their names or initials here.**

Family members:

Friends:

Because most people are led to trust Christ by friends and family, witnessing to your family and friends is incredibly important. If you see a car coming that may hit a friend, are you going to yell, "Look out"? Would you let the car hit him because you don't want a loud yell to startle anyone? Hell is real. Are you going to warn him, or do you choose to say nothing and let your friend go to hell?

> Because most people are led to trust Christ
> by friends and family, witnessing to your family
> and friends is incredibly important.

Some people have a fear of being ridiculed or persecuted. But Americans rarely experience the persecution that occurs in other countries. One reason is that Christians do not look or sound enough like Jesus. Isn't it worth the risk of ridicule or even persecution to tell a lost person about Jesus?

**Which fears are preventing you from witnessing?
Check all that apply.**

❑ **Fear of rejection**

❑ **Fear of not knowing enough**

❑ **Fear of offending**

❑ **Fear of ridicule or persecution**

Circle your greatest fear.

To give in to any of these fears is to practice the sin of silence. Henry Maxwell asked his congregation, "Is it not true that the call has come in this age for a new exhibition of Christian discipleship? What is the test of Christian discipleship? Is it not the same as in Christ's own time? Have our surroundings modified or changed the test? What would be the result if in this city every church member should begin to do as Jesus would do?"[2] Maxwell challenged his congregation with the challenge we too face in evangelism: "It is the personal element that Christian discipleship needs to emphasize. 'The gift without the giver is bare.' … There is not a different path today from that of Jesus' own times. It is the same path."[3]

You don't have to be afraid. Resist the temptation to count your weaknesses and believe they are unchangeable. Honestly share your fears of witnessing with God in prayer. Focus your heart on the strength that matters—the presence of God and assurance of His power.

It is not your strengths that will bring you the power to share Jesus with a lost person. It is your dependence on His power. Successful witnessing is about obedience and dependence. Your greatest strength is your willingness to trust God as your partner in guiding a lost brother or sister, parent, son or daughter, colleague at work, or stranger to know God's saving grace.

> It is not your strengths that will bring you the power to share Jesus with a lost person. It is your dependence on His power.

After years of experiencing God's care while facing the threats of enemies and the trials of life, David sang a song of praise in which he said,

> God is my strong refuge;
> He makes my way perfect.
> He makes my feet like the feet of a deer
> and sets me securely on the heights (2 Sam. 22:33-34).

David had this disposition toward God from the time he was a young boy tending flocks of sheep on Judean hillsides. As a young shepherd boy, many years before he sang this song of praise, David saw the soldiers of Saul running in fear, being humiliated by Goliath, a Philistine giant. David said to Saul, "Don't let anyone be discouraged by him; your servant will go and fight this Philistine!" (1 Sam. 17:32). Saul pointed out the reasons that David should fear the giant: "You're just a youth, and he's been a warrior since he was young" (1 Sam. 17:33). David described to Saul the dangers he had faced when lions and bears attacked flocks of sheep. He assured Saul, "The LORD who rescued me from the paw of the lion and the paw of the bear will rescue me from the hand of this Philistine" (1 Sam. 17:37).

David recognized that his success lay in the power of God. He faced the giant with all God had provided for him. He announced to the world that though Goliath was coming against him "with a dagger, spear, and sword," David was coming "in the name of the LORD of Hosts" (1 Sam. 17:45).

Today as you share Jesus without fear, know that you will go in the power of that same strong name—the Lord Almighty.

Spend time in prayer. Confess to God your fears about witnessing. Claim the promise of His presence and strength as you share the truth of Jesus Christ.

1. Harold F. Leestma, *More than a Spectator* (Glendale: Regal Books, 1974), 1. Used by permission.

2. Charles M. Sheldon, *In His Steps* (Nashville: Broadman & Holman, 1995), 232–34.

3. Ibid.

LEARNING
A WAY
TO SHARE JESUS

People love to express their opinions, and many are hungry to talk about their spiritual questions. Why do you think this is true?

_____

Opening (2 minutes)

- Turn to page 37 and ask group members to share their responses to this statement: People love to express their opinions, and many are hungry to talk about their spiritual questions. Why do you think this is true?
- Today we will learn five questions to determine where God is working.

DVD (7:10 minutes)

- View the first DVD segment on the five opening questions, "A Way to Share Jesus: Part 1." When the screen instructs you, stop.

  Five questions to determine where God is working:

  1. Do you have any kind of spiritual belief?
  2. To you, who is Jesus?
  3. Do you believe there are a heaven and a hell?
  4. If you died right now, where would you go?
  5. If what you believe were not true, would you want to know it?

Facilitator-Led Conversation (15 minutes)

- Model asking the five questions. Enlist someone in the group to role-play a person who is an unbeliever, portraying himself before coming to Christ or someone with whom he is thinking about sharing the gospel. The facilitator will play the part of someone sharing his faith. Respond to the answers only with "Umm" and "Uh-huh."
- Remind the group to recall what Bill Fay taught on the DVD and to watch the role play, listening for answers to the following questions.
  1. What am I doing to avoid an argument?
  2. What am I not doing?
- When the role play is completed, ask:
  1. How did I avoid an argument? (Asked questions.) Questions defuse defensiveness. When you try to tell people about your faith, often their defense is better than what you have to say. Asking questions works because people will share their opinions on most subjects.

2. What was I not doing? (Answering, commenting, or arguing.)
No matter what the person says, respond with "Umm" or
"Uh-huh." Listen but do not react or correct.

- Now ask participants to work in pairs to role-play using the five questions.
Ask one person to be the Christian who will read each of the five questions. The other person should answer the questions in the role of an
unbeliever. They should then reverse their roles and repeat the activity.

DVD (8 minutes) 10/28 start pt.

- View the second DVD segment on using the Bible, "A Way to Share
Jesus: Part 2." When the screen instructs you, stop.

Facilitator-Led Conversation (10 minutes)

- Discuss the two principles for how to use Scripture:
  1. Read it aloud.
  2. Ask, "What does it say to you?"

Remember: The lost person will read aloud. The lost person will talk.
The Holy Spirit will convince. God's Word will convict.

Video (7:45 minutes)

- View the third DVD segment with testimonies, "A Way to Share Jesus:
Part 3." When the screen instructs you, stop.

Closing (2 minutes)

- Use these five questions this week to determine how open people are
to Jesus' message. Use these questions with your neighbor, a relative,
a schoolmate, your barber or hairdresser, a delivery person, or others.
- Complete week 2 in the workbook. Bring your sharing New Testament
with you to the next session. (Share Jesus Without Fear New Testament
is recommended. See p. 112 and the inside back cover of this book.)
- Prayer.

There are three steps in sharing your faith

and guiding a lost person to Jesus:

1. A series of five questions that will help you discover the person's

spiritual condition

2. A series of Bible verses to ask the lost person to read aloud

3. A series of five questions that summarize the truths of the verses

and lead the lost person to the point of decision

During the next two weeks you will learn how to use these simple steps to guide a lost person to Christ. At the same time, your own relationship with Christ will be strengthened.

This week you will be introduced to the first of the three steps. You will learn five questions that will help you discover a person's spiritual condition. These are only guides and are not intended to begin a theological debate.

The second step in sharing your faith consists of seven Bible verses. Beginning with Romans 3:23 and concluding with Revelation 3:20, this seven-verse series will be read aloud by the non-Christian. After each verse you will ask the unbeliever, "What does this verse say to you?" Then you will wait for the Holy Spirit to convict his or her heart.

#3 In the third step you will again find five questions. These will summarize the truths of the verses from step 2 and will lead the person to the ultimate question: "Are you ready to invite Jesus into your heart and your life?"

Following these steps will help you avoid unnecessary arguments or defensiveness that can be hindrances. Two important facts will encourage you:

1. This method makes witnessing incredibly simple.

2. You absolutely, unconditionally, and positively cannot fail.

Can you recall from week 1 the reason you cannot fail when witnessing? Write your answer here.

It is not my job to "cause" conversion

Remember, success is living the Christian life daily, sharing the gospel, and trusting God for the results. Successful witnessing occurs the moment you are obedient to respond and to share. Learning to witness is more about learning to trust and obey God than it is about improving your skills or learning the right methods. Witnessing is more about obedience than measuring success by results. You don't have to fear what may go wrong when you attempt to guide someone to trust Jesus as Savior and Lord. Your part is to be obedient to witness. Fear of witnessing is more about your own uneasiness than it is about the lost person's objections. Failure is not possible when you are faithful. When you witness to a lost person in partnership with the Holy Spirit, you will be amazed by His power to break down all barriers. You will say, "I wish I had known how to do this before."

DAY 1

PREPARATION FOR SHARING YOUR FAITH

One Wednesday evening I had left my office and was driving home on a dark, winding road. As I came around a corner, several police cars and a Flight for Life helicopter were directly in front of me. A Volkswagen had smashed into a tree, and the 19-year-old driver would have to be cut out of the twisted wreckage. Emergency medical personnel were inserting IVs into his arms to stabilize him. As I looked into the circle of the emergency medical workers, God spoke to me. I pushed my way through the crowd, knelt down close to driver, and asked him to respond if he could hear me. He couldn't speak, but he groaned in agreement. I knew I had only seconds before he would be taken away. I said, "If you can say yes from your heart to these five questions, God will enter your life today." I then asked, "Are you a sinner?" He indicated yes with a groan.

"Do you want forgiveness for your sins?" He indicated yes.

"Do you believe Jesus died on the cross for you and rose again?" Another indication of yes.

"Are you willing to surrender yourself to Christ?" He groaned a weak yes.

"Do you want Jesus Christ to come into your life and into your heart?" And finally a fifth groan. This young man, in critical condition, accepted Christ at that moment.

He died the next day.

I know this fact: if this young man's yes was from his heart, he is a young man walking the streets of gold today and saying, "Wow! That was close!" I was so glad I was prepared to share the simplicity of the gospel. You will also be glad when you have learned to share Jesus without fear.

Learning to share Jesus does not mean an absence of fear. It means being prepared to respond to witnessing opportunities with those who otherwise have no hope of salvation. Witnessing without fear means not letting fears dictate your choice of obedience in sharing Jesus with a lost person. You must look away from the causes of fear and look to the source of power, saying with the apostle Paul, "When I came to you, brothers, announcing the testimony of God to you, I did not come with brilliance of speech or wisdom. For I determined to know nothing among you except Jesus Christ and Him crucified. And I was with you in weakness, in fear, and in much trembling. My speech and my proclamation were not with persuasive words of wisdom, but with a demonstration of the Spirit and power, so that your faith might not be based on men's wisdom but on God's power" (1 Cor. 2:1-5).

With faith in God and His Word, you can successfully witness without fear of failure. Once you have discovered a passion for the lost, adequately prepared yourself through prayer, and realized your partnership with God, the Holy Spirit will provide the power.

Take a moment to visualize the faces of family members, friends, and acquaintances who are lost. Pray for these and pray for yourself. Pray that as you progress through this week's study, God will burden your heart and guide your will to respond to witnessing opportunities.

As you continue in this study, you will learn a comfortable way to discover the spiritual needs of lost people you know and to share your faith with them.

Peter wrote, "Always be ready to give a defense to anyone who asks you for a reason for the hope that is in you" (1 Pet. 3:15). God will never force you to be obedient. However, if you have a desire to obey Him, He will provide a way through all the obstacles that may hinder you from witnessing.

Satan wants nothing more than to cause you to be silent when God is working in the life of a lost person. A Christian witness must recognize the character and intent of Satan, the nature of the confrontation with him, and its significance. Satan shrewdly works to discourage you from doing anything that will honor and bring advantage to God. He is a subtle but great discourager. It is easy for Satan to discourage you against witnessing, because the protests seem so reasonable.

Do you think Satan has used discouragement to prevent you from witnessing? ❏ Yes   ❏ No   If so, how?

The struggle with Satan is not one you can win in your own power. You must "be strong in the Lord and in His mighty power" (Eph. 6:10, NIV). All Satan can do is not strong enough to make your witness a failure, "because the One who is in you is greater than the one who is in the world" (1 John 4:4).

> ## "The One who is in you is greater than the one who is in the world."
>
> 1 JOHN 4:4

On a flight from Denver to Newark, I had been preoccupied with reading until just before we landed. A woman next to me had also been reading, and just before landing, she closed her book. I asked, "Is this the end of your travel today?" She replied, "Yes." I asked, "What do you do for a living?" She replied that she was an engineer for a large corporation. I said, "That's great."

Then I asked her one of the best questions to turn a conversation to Christian concerns: "Do you go to church anywhere?" This simple question often elicits predictable responses. One response I get is something like "My third cousin in Nebraska is a pastor." But the person can never remember the name of the church where he serves. Another popular response is "I go to the big, white church where I live"; but the person can't remember the name of the church or the pastor.

This woman quickly said, "Yes, I'm a Coptic Catholic." Her answer told me that she went to a church that combined Greek Orthodoxy and Roman Catholicism. My next question was one I had never asked before: "How does a Coptic Catholic become saved?" As the plane chugged along for about two minutes before arriving at the gate, she said, "I wish someone would tell me how I could be saved."

I had an opportunity to witness to a person whom God had prepared to hear the gospel. It was clear that she was open to God's work in her heart. But we had only seconds before we would reach the terminal gate, and I couldn't see how I would have the time to do what God wanted. Suddenly, the pilot came on the speaker system and announced, "Sorry, ladies and gentlemen, we can't go to the gate right now. There is a plane at our gate. It will be about 10 minutes." My heart was pounding with excitement. It was as if the hand of God reached down and stopped everything. This woman wanted to hear, and I was not afraid to share.

I later realized how easily I had forgotten who is in control. God is. Not me. Not circumstance. God is at work in the hearts of people everywhere, and I cannot fail if I will not be silent. During this delay while others fretted, I rejoiced to have the privilege of guiding an openhearted engineer to accept Jesus as the Savior and Lord of her life.

Any conversation can be turned into an opportunity to share the gospel. The approach in this study does not require you to set aside two hours each week to do evangelism. This approach enables you to move through your normal patterns of life, always ready to be obedient as God gives you opportunities.

As a Christian, you should be ready to share your personal journey to salvation—a brief, three-minute description of what your life was like before you met Christ (one minute), how you became a Christian (one minute), and the difference Christ has made in your life (one minute). It is helpful to prepare in advance so that you will be able to share your testimony easily when the opportunity arises.

Briefly describe the way you came to Jesus. State clearly and simply what Christ has done in your life.

What your life was like before you met Christ:

not much $

*1) Late 20's - working like crazy,
lonely, "what's it all for?"
Kept making bad decisions*

*Say something
ask question
listen
+ hook of Spirit
+ truth
Conversation that
way*

How you became a Christian:

The difference Christ has made in your life:

As you prepare to share your testimony, keep in mind two things.

1. A testimony is not an argument. Sharing Jesus must be motivated by a loving desire to guide a lost person from darkness to light and from hopelessness to hope. It must not be motivated by a desire merely to prove a lost person wrong.

2. A testimony must be supported by a Christian lifestyle. Be consistent in living the faith you proclaim, "keeping your conscience clear, so that when you are accused, those who denounce your Christian life will be put to shame" (1 Pet. 3:16). Consistent Christian living substantiates your testimony and gives credibility to your witness. It is difficult for a lost person to believe the claims of a Christian whose life runs contrary to the standards of Christ.

USE QUESTIONS THAT DETERMINE WHERE GOD IS WORKING

The first step in sharing your faith is a series of five questions that will help you determine someone's spiritual condition. These questions will reveal valuable information that will help you sense how God is working in the person's life. Asking questions will also help you avoid talking more than you listen. It is essential to listen to what God is saying to the person through Scripture. Allow the Holy Spirit to touch the person's heart with conviction.

Have you ever used a meat thermometer when cooking at home? If you are like me, you put the probe inside the roast because you don't know what is going on in there. I can't constantly watch my roast as it cooks. Sometimes it cooks fast, and sometimes it cooks slowly. So I use a meat thermometer.

Questions serve as a kind of spiritual-condition thermometer in witnessing. They provide a way to sense what is going on in a lost person's heart and mind. You can use questions to direct any conversation to a test of spiritual temperature.

While I was in an airport waiting area, I talked with a young man who asked me whether a flight had been delayed. After casual talk about where he was headed, I said, "Sir, what is your favorite sport?" He replied that he was a big NBA basketball fan. I said, "Wow, it's something the money some of those guys are making. I just heard that one player signed a deal for many millions of dollars for several years. In spite of their success, every now and then you pick up the sports page, and some player has trashed his life. And yet he is making so much money. Do you ever wonder how much money a man has to make before his life is OK? For me, as long as my family is healthy and safe, I've got a decent job, and the family is involved in the life of our church, then life is great. Is your family active in a church anywhere?"

Notice the natural way the conversation moved to the topic of the Christian life. This young man and I went from basketball to his spiritual life. One question turned the conversation to deeper thoughts in an instant.

A woman talked with me after a meeting I attended. I asked, "What do you think is the biggest problem women face today?" She thought for a moment and replied, "Too much to do and not enough hours in a day to do it." I replied, "I don't see how women do it. I'm not convinced that a 40-hour week would do it for you. With all of the sensitive, God-created emotions He has given you, do you ever have time just to stop and think about life and what the really important things are? I mean, do you ever have time just to stop and wonder about life and what would happen to you if all this activity suddenly stopped and you died?"

Do you see the way questions allowed me to naturally change the direction of the conversation? Questions serve as an excellent probe to reveal what is going on spiritually in a person.

Five questions can help you move a conversation toward spiritual concerns:

1. Do you have any kind of spiritual belief?
2. To you, who is Jesus?
3. Do you believe there are a heaven and a hell?
4. If you died right now, where would you go?
5. If what you believe were not true, would you want to know it?

The acrostic SALT will remind you to look for ways to turn any conversation toward witnessing:

S reminds you to say something.

A reminds you to ask questions, which is a way to find out how God is at work in the person's heart.

L reminds you to listen, which is the best way to learn what's going on and gain the opportunity to accomplish your goal.

T reminds you to turn the conversation to spiritual thought. You will see how easy it is to turn any conversation into a spiritual conversation.[1]

Fill in the blanks to complete the key words in the SALT acrostic.

S _say_ .

A _ask_ .

L _listen_ .

T _think_ (Turn) **the conversation to** _spiritual_ _thing_ .

Question 1: Do you have any kind of spiritual belief?

Write your own response to question 1 and elaborate briefly.

It is important to begin where people are, not where you wish they were. Most of us no longer live in a predominantly churched culture. Most lost people today have much less understanding of what a Christian witness is talking about than in past generations. Questions such as "Do you believe in God?" and "Are you a Christian?" can cause immediate defensiveness in a lost person.

> ## Questions such as "Do you believe in God?" and "Are you a Christian?" can cause immediate defensiveness in a lost person.

A question such as "Do you believe in God?" may be too personal and direct. But when you ask, "Do you have any kind of spiritual belief?" most people feel freedom to express their opinions without being pinned down. It is broad enough to allow people to bring their disbelief into the conversation. People love to express their opinions, and many are hungry to talk about their spiritual questions. They often hide this hunger behind false indifference or terse answers. Nevertheless, they are hungry and seek ways to talk safely about spiritual things. Question 1 sets the stage for talking about Jesus.

Read Acts 8:26-39 in your Bible. What question did Philip ask the Ethiopian?

Why do you think Philip asked this question?

The Holy Spirit sent Philip to a desert road going from Jerusalem to Gaza. He encountered a man from Ethiopia who was returning home. Philip asked, "Do you understand what you're reading?" (Acts 8:30). The Ethiopian responded with a question that allowed Philip immediately to focus the conversation on Jesus: "Philip proceeded to tell him the good news about Jesus, beginning from that Scripture" (Acts 8:35).

Whether the person answers yes or no to your first question, it is important to let him or her talk. It doesn't matter whether the person replies for 10 seconds or 10 minutes. You should not respond or attempt to clarify anything he says. Focus on attentive listening, which is an act of love and care. Your only response should be something like "Umm" or "Uh-huh." The person will have nothing to argue or be defensive about if the only requirement is to talk about his feelings, beliefs, and opinions.

Be open to many opportunities God will provide to use this question with relatives, coworkers, neighbors, and other acquaintances. Also be sensitive to others who cross your daily path.

Can you think of people in your life whom you could ask this question? Write some names or initials here.

Start looking for opportunities to ask question 1 in your daily routine.

QUESTIONS 2 AND 3

Question 2: To you, who is Jesus?

Take a moment to write your own response to question 2.

Read Matthew 21:10-11. What question did the people ask?

When Jesus entered the city of Jerusalem, the people were moved and asked, "Who is this?" (v. 10). This hunger in the minds and hearts of people is still alive today. For this reason you should find a way to introduce question 2, "To you, who is Jesus?" into the conversation quickly. This is the question that really matters. It is the one question that will open the lost person's heart like no other.

Read Matthew 16:13-16. What questions did Jesus ask?

Jesus pushed to the heart of what mattered: " 'What about you?' He asked, 'Who do you say that I am?' " (v. 15, NIV). Everyone must answer this same question. Bringing this question to the forefront of the conversation is key to guiding a lost person to Christ.

> ## "Who do you say that I am?"
> MATTHEW 16:15, NIV

Read John 8:12-30. How did Jesus identify Himself?
- ❏ **The Bread of life**
- ❏ **The Resurrection and the Life**
- ❏ **The Light of the world**

How did the Pharisees react to Jesus' claim?

What did Jesus say would happen to them if they refused to believe in Him?

Many people can identify Jesus as the subject of the New Testament yet do not know Him personally. In John 8 Jesus declared the necessity of knowing His true identity. Jesus told them, "I am the light of the world. Anyone who follows Me will never walk in the darkness but will have the light of life" (v. 12).

The Pharisees challenged Jesus' claim to have come from God (see v. 13) and spiritually stumbled when they were asked to believe in Him as the only way of salvation. Jesus said, "I'm going away; you will look for Me, and you will die in your sin. Where I'm going, you cannot come" (v. 21). He warned them, "You are from below; I am from above. You are of this world; I am not of this world. I told you that you would die in your sins; if you do not believe that I am the one I claim to be, you will indeed die in your sins" (John 8:23-24, NIV). The Pharisees refusal to believe that Jesus was one with the Father meant they were going to die in their sins. What was true for them is true for everyone.

When you ask, "To you, who is Jesus?" some people will answer, "The Son of God" or "The man who died on the cross." Notice that such answers are religious but do not indicate a personal relationship. A Christian would simply answer, "My Savior and Lord."

A lost person may want to know that you have a personal relationship with Jesus. For you to say, "He is my Savior and Lord" will provide a powerful opportunity for the Holy Spirit to speak to the lost person.

Your best response after asking, "To you, who is Jesus?" is to say nothing. The purpose is to cause the other person to think about Jesus and to allow an opportunity for the Holy Spirit to continue convicting him of his spiritual emptiness. The purpose is not to teach a lesson or convince him of something. That is the role of Scripture and the Holy Spirit. The Holy Spirit will speak to the lost person's heart. Remember, it's your role to be obedient. You must respect each individual's freedom to say yes or no to Jesus.

Question 3: Do you believe there are a heaven and a hell?

Write your own response to this question.

Question 3 is also a nonthreatening question. You are not asking the person to say yes or no about his own destiny. However, you are opening an opportunity for him to talk about the subject. Lost people will often talk freely about what they believe and don't believe about the life to come.

Jesus didn't ignore the existence of hell, nor did He dwell on it. It is not a good idea to focus the entire thrust of your witness on the consequences of rejecting Christ. It is a worse idea to leave out the subject altogether.

Read Luke 16:19-31. Check the statement that holds more value for today's witness.
- ❏ **A discussion of hell will encourage people to accept Jesus.**
- ❏ **Lost people will come to Jesus when they recognize who He is.**

Using the story of the rich man and Lazarus, Jesus taught that vivid descriptions and proofs of hell will not necessarily lead a person to accept Jesus in faith. The rich man pleaded for Lazarus to be sent from heaven to tell his brothers what heaven and hell are like: "I beg you to send him to my father's house—because I have five brothers—to warn them, so they won't also come to this place of torment" (Luke 16:27-28). Abraham's reply was that they had as much warning as was necessary: "He told him, 'If they don't listen to Moses and the prophets, they will not be persuaded if someone rises from the dead' " (Luke 16:31).

Recognizing who Jesus is and placing faith in Him as Savior and Lord are the goals of a witnessing encounter. Ask questions 2 and 3 and let people tell you what they believe. Let the Holy Spirit use these questions to turn their hearts toward Jesus.

4 QUESTIONS 4 AND 5

Question 4: If you died right now, where would you go?

**Take a moment to write your own response to this question.
Also state why you answered as you did.**

A woman once responded quickly to question 3, "Do you think there are a heaven and a hell?" with an emphatic "Absolutely not." When she was asked this question, it became personal. But when asked, "Where would you go?" she immediately said, "Heaven, of course."

How would you explain the woman's contradictory answers?

The third question calls for an intellectual response. The fourth question, on the other hand, requires a response from the heart, causing the person to become more personal. People get very serious when they reflect on personal aspects of their lives.

People get very serious when they reflect on personal aspects of their lives.

Most lost people are determined not to expose their vulnerability to probing people. The conversational approach breaks down this barrier by immediately allowing the relationship to grow. I have sat beside people on airplanes who introduced themselves by saying they don't talk much, meaning they don't intend to. After a time, however, I am amazed by the deeply personal things they introduce in a discussion.

Lost people are far more aware of and sensitive to their lostness and fears of spiritual brokenness than we often recognize. Those who seem most confident in their unbelief may actually be the most sensitive if approached in the right way.

If someone answers question 4 with "Heaven," ask, "Why would God let you into heaven?" The answer will open his or her heart to additional truth.

Question 5: If what you believe were not true, would you want to know it?

Write your own response to this question and explain why you answered this way.

Question 5 is a crucial question. People fear missing opportunities because of not knowing the right information.

Jesus was willing to ask the hard questions when the time was right. Following His example, you must be direct and clear as a person comes to the point of understanding what it means to accept Christ as Savior and Lord.

This is a crucial point in the witnessing process. There are only two possible answers to question 5, yes or no. If the answer is yes, you proceed to step 2 (reading Bible verses aloud; see week 3). If the answer is no, stop. I have had people answer no, but I have never had a no that stuck. When people say no, I do nothing. Silence often creates a lot of conversation. Most say something like "Well, aren't you going to tell me?" I jokingly say, "No, you didn't want to know." They say yes, and the door opens for me to continue.

If you get a firm no, however, remember that the person's choice is not your responsibility. He or she is using the freedom of choice that God gives. This response reflects no failure on your part. You have been faithful and obedient.

Read 2 Peter 3:9 on this page. Why does God delay Jesus' return?

> "The Lord does not delay His promise,
> as some understand delay, but is patient
> with you, not wanting any to perish,
> but all to come to repentance."
>
> 2 PETER 3:9

The delay of Jesus' second coming provides more opportunities for lost people to accept Christ. If the lost person says no to you, God may provide additional opportunities for him or her to accept Christ. You can be sure that God is patient, not wanting anyone to be lost. Yet they always remain free to choose to be saved or to choose to reject Him.

Many people have had an experience that confronted them with their need to accept Jesus. Paul had this kind of experience while walking on the road to Damascus (see Acts 9:3-19). Many others seem to find Christ through a series of events or experiences. Others hear that they must look to Jesus in faith for forgiveness of sin; yet they still refuse. A Christian who witnesses must not consider the effort a failure if the person does not accept Christ. Be patient. Your witness may be the experience that causes the lost person to open his heart to Christ during his next encounter with the Holy Spirit.

Suppose that you enter a restaurant and Karen invites you to sit at her table. The conversation turns to your involvement in a nearby church:

> **Karen: "I've thought about going to church, but I keep putting it off."**
>
> **You: "Well, I would really love for you to come with me. How about next Sunday?"**
>
> **Karen: "No, not next Sunday. Perhaps another time. I'm not a Christian or anything. I might try it someday."**

The door of opportunity is open at this moment. Check the way you would respond.

- ❏ **Continue to try to talk Karen into attending church with you next Sunday.**
- ❏ **Ask for the Holy Spirit to help you as you use the first five questions to guide your friend, gently and courteously, to faith in Jesus Christ.**
- ❏ **Change the subject.**

A gentle, caring acceptance of a person's decision to deny Christ will likely provide a future opportunity, either for you or for someone else. If you are patient to build the relationship you have begun, you may open the door to additional opportunities. Remember that the Holy Spirit must bring this person to salvation. It is a great comfort to know that when our witness seems to have been rejected, the Holy Spirit patiently continues to convict, convince, and love the individual.

Share the opening questions with at least one person this week.

For
_10/28_

DAY

5 LET THE BIBLE SPEAK

The second step in sharing Jesus without fear is to allow the Bible to speak. God uses Scripture to change people's lives. Learn to let the Bible speak to the hearts of people.

This step provides a series of Bible verses to ask the lost person to read aloud:

1. Romans 3:23   _1_
2. Romans 6:23   _2_
3. John 3:3   _6_
4. John 14:6   _4_
5. Romans 10:9-11   _5_
6. 2 Corinthians 5:15   _3_
7. Revelation 3:20   _7_

or John Rodgers
suggested this order

Stop and read the preceding verses in your Bible. Why do you think they are important for a lost person to read?

The ultimate intention in asking the five opening questions in the first step is to get the person to read the New Testament verses that make up the second step. You will rarely experience resistance from a lost person while you are asking the first five questions. If the lost person is going to be defensive or resistant, it will likely be when you pull out your New Testament.

Two negative remarks about the Bible are most common:

1. "There are many errors in the Bible." The most effective response I have used is to hand the person my Bible and say, with all the love I can muster, "You know, I've been reading this for many years. I wonder, could you be kind enough to show me one of those errors?" The person always admits that he really doesn't know of any errors but has only heard other people talk about them. Respond by lovingly saying, "Well, I've heard those

opinions, but I've never found any evidence." I immediately say, "Let's turn to Romans 3:23." Don't make a bigger issue of the remark.

2. "There are many translations of Scripture. How do you know which one is right?" I answer this way: "Yes. That's right. There are many translations and paraphrases, including the King James Version, the New King James Version, the New International Version, the Holman Christian Standard Bible, the New American Standard Bible, and more." I add, "Did you know that each of these Christian versions all share the same content?" People often reply, "No, I didn't know that." I say, "For a while I didn't know it either. Let's turn to Romans 3:23." I ask him or her immediately to read the verse aloud. No one has ever refused.

For two thousand years men and women have examined the Bible, some to prove it true and some to prove it false. It has been proved true many times. Not once has it been proved false. God brought the Bible without error through imperfect human writers. You can trust the Bible. God will pour out His power through its reading. You can trust God to speak through it.

Two important principles will guide you to use Bible verses in sharing your faith.

1. Hearing. It is important to say, "Read the verse aloud."

Read Romans 10:17 on this page. How does faith come?
From _hearing the message_

How is the message heard? Through the _word of Christ._

"Faith comes from hearing the message, and the message is heard through the word of Christ."

ROMANS 10:17, NIV

Faith comes from hearing. Hearing is the key. There are practical reasons you want the person to read the Bible aloud:

- When a lost person hears the message of the Bible, he is hearing Christ Himself, who speaks the message of salvation.
- You want to ensure that the person is reading the right verse. Someone who is not familiar with the Bible might read the wrong verse. His reading aloud assures you that he is hearing the correct message.

2. **Question.** When the person has finished reading the verse, it is important for you to ask, "What does this say to you?" Read Luke 10:25-26: "Just then an expert in the law stood up to test Him, saying, 'Teacher, what must I do to inherit eternal life?' 'What is written in the law?' He asked him. 'How do you read it?' " God's Word does all of the convicting. The Holy Spirit does all of the convincing. You are in the page-turning business at this point. You have one goal: to stay out of God's way. Stand by and watch God work. Listen to what the Scripture says to the lost person. Your only response should be something like "Umm" or "Uh-huh."

Remember:
- The lost person does the reading aloud.
- The lost person does the talking. Listen in a way that encourages him or her to talk.
- The Holy Spirit does the convincing.
- God's Word does the convicting.

"When He comes, He will convict the world about sin, righteousness, and judgment: about sin, because they do not believe in Me; about righteousness, because I am going to the Father and you will no longer see Me; and about judgment, because the ruler of this world has been judged."

JOHN 16:8-11

Read John 16:8-11 on the previous page. What is the Holy Spirit's role in regard to sin?

1) Convicting
2) that : sin = unbelief that
J : righteousness = Jesus is ℝ → the Father
+ Now with
: judgement = the evil ruler of the world is already condemned

It is the work of the Holy Spirit to convict and convince people of their sinfulness and need for salvation through Jesus Christ. Therefore, you cannot fail when you witness. Let the Spirit and the Word bring conviction in the lost person's heart.

Sometimes when Christians begin looking at verses to use in witnessing, they become afraid and think, *Wow, I will never be able to memorize all of the verses*. The card attached to the back cover of this workbook will help you.

Find and tear out the card with the questions and Scriptures at the back of this book. Carry it with you to review during the week.

There is nothing wrong with referring to a small card with the verses that will guide a person to eternal life. God will bless your faithfulness in introducing them to the lost person. After you have shared Jesus a few times, using the verses will seem automatic. The process—asking questions and waiting as the Holy Spirit convinces and convicts through the reading of the Scriptures—soon develops naturally through normal conversation.

Next week you will need a pocket-sized New Testament during the training session.[2] Day 1's activities will teach you how to mark your New Testament so that you can walk someone through the key verses, have them read the verses aloud, and ask them, "What does this say to you?"

---

1. Adapted from Alan Nelson, *Five-Minute Ministry* (Grand Rapids: Baker Books, 1993), 41–49.

2. An inexpensive New Testament recommended for witnessing is *Share Jesus Without Fear New Testament*. See page 112 and the inside back cover of this book.

RESPONDING TO THE
CHALLENGE
TO SHARE JESUS

Are you prepared to perform CPR or the Heimlich maneuver on someone in an emergency situation?

Have you ever used one of these techniques to save someone's life?

What preparation is needed to share the gospel?

SMALL-GROUP EXPERIENCE | **SESSION 3**

Opening (15 minutes)

- Turn to page 63 and ask group members to share their responses to these questions: Are you prepared to perform CPR or the Heimlich maneuver on someone in an emergency situation? Have you ever used one of these techniques to save someone's life? What preparation is needed to share the gospel?

- Read 1 Corinthians 2:3-5: "I was with you in weakness, in fear, and in much trembling. My speech and my proclamation were not with persuasive words of wisdom, but with a demonstration of the Spirit and power, so that your faith might not be based on men's wisdom but on God's power."

- Ask group members to share their experiences using the five questions.

- If your church is providing New Testaments, distribute one to each person present. An inexpensive New Testament recommended for witnessing is *Share Jesus Without Fear New Testament* (see p. 112 and the inside back cover of this book). Encourage participants to mark their New Testaments this week, following the instructions in week 3, day 1.

DVD (14:15 minutes)

- View the first DVD segment, "A Way to Share Jesus: Part 1."

- Seven verses are given in the summary on letting the Bible speak:
  1. Romans 3:23
  2. Romans 6:23
  3. John 3:3
  4. John 14:6
  5. Romans 10:9-11
  6. 2 Corinthians 5:15
  7. Revelation 3:20

Matthew

- Let the Bible speak.
- Here are phrases for each verse from Bill Fay's summary:

Romans 3:23 — The issue of sin ✓ *vs. Gift*

Romans 6:23 — The penalty of sin ✓ → *in Christ not in religion.*

John 3:3 *Bkpt.* — How to enter a relationship with Christ *Be reborn*

John 14:6 — The narrowness of the gospel ✓

Romans 10:9-11 — Anyone can be saved.

2 Corinthians 5:15 — We must turn from/turn to (surrender). *Sunflower*

Revelation 3:20 — A choice to accept or reject *Your choice.*

Acts 3:

Matthew

Facilitator-Led Conversation (15 minutes)

- Ask pairs to role-play the verses, using the two principles: (1) hearing and (2) asking questions. These are discussed on pages 59–60. The first person in the role of the Christian will ask the other person to read aloud the first verse and ask, "What does it say to you?" (Suggest that the answers can be brief.) Reverse roles. The second person will do the same with the next verse. It is not necessary to role-play all seven verses for the participants to understand how to use these principles.
- Ask: *Why is it so difficult to trust in the power of the Holy Spirit and God's Word?*

Transition — 1) I know I'm a sinner — Do you think you are?
2) Know any perfect people.

DVD (3:30 minutes)

- View the DVD segment on the closing questions, "The Challenge." When the screen instructs you, stop.

If person stops the conversation Let it stop

- Five questions that lead to a point of decision:

1. Are you a sinner?
2. Do you want forgiveness for your sins?
3. Do you believe Jesus died on the cross for you and rose again?
4. Are you willing to surrender your life to Christ?
5. Are you ready to invite Jesus into your life and into your heart?

Facilitator-Led Conversation (10 minutes)

- Review the five questions that lead to a point of decision.
- Ask participants to work in pairs to role-play a scenario using the questions. Ask one person to be the Christian. He or she will read each of the five questions (listed on p. 65). The other person should answer the questions as an unbeliever might answer them. The two persons should then reverse roles and repeat the activity.
- What are the two most important behaviors for a witness after asking the fifth question?
- Why is it important after the fifth question to be silent and pray?
- Prayer: "Heavenly Father, I have sinned against You. I want forgiveness of all my sins. I believe Jesus died on the cross for me and rose again. Father, I give You my life to do with as You wish. I want Jesus Christ to come into my life and into my heart. I ask this in Jesus' name. Amen."
- Notice how the suggested prayer and the five questions correspond.

DVD (10:45 minutes)

- View the third DVD segment on objections and the why principle, "The Challenge: Part 2." When the screen instructs you, stop.

Facilitator-Led Conversation (6 minutes)

- Bill Fay identifies the following objections that people may offer when they come to a point of decision about receiving Christ as their Savior:
  1. "I'm not ready yet."
  2. "There are too many hypocrites in the church."
  3. "I enjoy my sinful life."
  4. "I'm not good enough."
  5. "There are many religions in the world, and I don't know how a person can determine which one is right."

- What is the best one-word response to objections for praying to receive Christ?
- Is there an objection that cannot be isolated by the why principle?
- Why is it important to use the why principle rather than trying to answer an unbeliever's objections?
- Add: The purpose of the why principle is to identify and discover the real issue. You can keep using "Why?" to get to the real issue.
- Refer to "36 Responses to Objections" on pages 98–108. Encourage participants to read these ideas and to use them when they encounter objections.

DVD (7:15 minutes)

- View the fourth DVD segment with the testimonies, "The Challenge: Part 3." When the screen instructs you, stop.

Facilitator-Led Conversation (4 minutes)

- Share the names of persons they plan to share the gospel with this week.

Closing (2 minutes)

- Plan appointments for this week with those you have listed. Be prepared to share your meetings with the group next week.
- Complete week 3 in the workbook.
- Lead the group in praying specifically for each person listed.

Who needs the gospel around us?
- Some stranger? → ask the Lord.
- a family member → Panama ··· Canada ···
- an acquaintance → Andree's children
- or neighbor? → all far away.
  - Albrechts?

Someone once told me to be prepared for any opportunity. You never know when your preparation may save someone's life. This advice became clear to me when a man suddenly stood up at a restaurant, knocking a glass off the table. He held his arms up and was struggling to breathe. Food had become lodged in his throat, and his panicked wife was unable to respond in any way.

I glanced around the room, hoping someone would quickly go to him and apply the Heimlich maneuver. But everyone else was also looking around for help. No one was responding. The man was beginning to stumble, so I went to him and applied the maneuver. The food immediately dislodged, and I could hear the welcome sound of a deep breath. Because I knew this maneuver, I was prepared to save this man's life.

Several people who had observed this event came by my table and expressed appreciation that I had helped the man. One gentleman said, "I'm so thankful that you knew what to do. Could you tell me where I could learn to do that? I've been thinking about what could have happened if no one had known what to do. I want to be prepared if something like that happens when I'm the only one around."

The man's wife left a note for me with the cashier. It said, "Thank you. My husband wanted to thank you but was too embarrassed and weak to say anything. We are so thankful that you weren't afraid to help us."

But no one could have been more afraid than I had been. It wasn't absence of fear that made the difference. I have a heart for helping people in need. I am confident that others in the room would have liked to help. The difference at that moment of opportunity was that I was prepared. Although I was afraid of failure, I was more afraid of not doing what I could, knowing the man's life depended on my action.

The same is true of a Christian witness. You might be the only hope for someone whose life hangs in the balance. Using the three steps in *Share Jesus Without Fear*, you can be prepared to save lives. The third step is the heart of the witnessing experience, leading a person into a lasting relationship with Christ.

#3 is

Remember that sharing your faith in Jesus does not mean absence of fear. It means being prepared to help people who have no hope if you don't respond. Someone's life may depend on your preparation and willingness to serve.

This is the part in the witnessing process that many Christians fear most. Asking for a decision is sometimes a great barrier to witnessing. Yet asking for a decision in favor of Christ should not be a time for fear. The power of the Holy Spirit will have worked in the life of the lost person. You can expect His power to be even more evident when the decision-making time has come.

Remember that sharing your faith in Jesus does not mean absence of fear. It means being prepared to help people who have no hope if you don't respond.

DAY 1

MARK YOUR NEW TESTAMENT

To be prepared for any witnessing opportunity, always keep a pocket-sized New Testament with you wherever you go.[1] This should be a version that can be easily understood by a non-Christian. Use this New Testament only for witnessing. Because your personal study Bible is probably marked, highlighted, and filled with notes, it could be distracting to a person who needs to focus on one or two verses, perhaps seeing them for the first time.

> ### To be prepared for any witnessing opportunity, always keep a pocket-sized New Testament with you wherever you go.

Today you will mark your New Testament so that you can walk someone through the key verses, have them read the verses aloud, and ask them, "What does this say to you?" Follow these directions to mark the New Testament you will use for witnessing. Use a colored highlighter to mark each verse. You will ask someone to take your Bible and read the verse, and the color will help him find it quickly.

1. **Highlight Romans 3:23**. In the top margin on this page in your Bible, write with a pen "Romans 6:23." Because I usually sit across from the person, I write the verse in the top margin and upside down. As the person reads Romans 3:23, you will see the reference for the next verse in the top margin. This will help you remember where to turn next.

2. **Highlight Romans 6:23** and circle the words *sin* and *death*. Also circle the word *in* (or *through* in some translations) preceding "Christ Jesus our Lord." Write "John 3:3" in the margin.

3. **Highlight John 3:3** and write "John 14:6" in the top margin. Draw a cross in the margin near John 3:3. Place an *X* beside the cross. Beside the cross you have drawn, write the question "Why did Jesus come to die?" The *X* reminds you that this is the only exception in the process. You don't want to ask, "What does this verse say to you?" after the person reads this verse

because you would apply unneeded pressure. Not many lost people know the answer to this question. He or she may feel unfairly placed on the spot.

4. **Highlight John 14:6** and write "Romans 10:9-11" in the top margin.

5. **Highlight Romans 10:9-11** and write "2 Corinthians 5:15" in the top margin.

6. **Highlight 2 Corinthians 5:15** and write "Revelation 3:20" in the top margin.

7. **Highlight Revelation 3:20.**

Locate the card you removed last week from the back of this workbook. Keep it in your pocket or in your Bible.

You don't have to be uncomfortable about referring to notes in the margin or to the card to find the verses you want to use. There is no evidence that lost people are more responsive to someone who seems to have the Bible verses memorized. Often a lost person is more comfortable knowing that a Christian is finding verses with help. Someone who is not a Christian will recognize that a person doesn't have to be an extraordinary scholar or student of Scripture to find the way to salvation, peace, and hope.

Now that you have marked a New Testament, you are ready to learn how to introduce the verses to lost people. You will use the two principles of hearing you learned last week ("Read the verse aloud") and questioning ("What does this verse say to you?") in this approach.

Verse 1: Romans 3:23

Ask the person to read Romans 3:23 aloud: "All have sinned and fall short of the glory of God." Point to the highlighted verse in your Bible. When the person has finished reading the verse, ask, "What does this verse say to you?"

Write your own response to this question.

The person will most likely answer your question with a statement like "Everyone has sinned." After listening, turn to Romans 6:23. There will be no argument or negative exchange. Why? Because you aren't pressing your interpretation. The Holy Spirit does all the convicting. You are in the page-turning business at this point. Your one goal is to stay out of God's way.

As the person talks about Romans 3:23, he may talk about sins he hasn't committed. He may defend himself as not having murdered, stolen, or done other dramatic things that are obvious sins. In this case you don't have to explain sin, but you may want to point out that the divine standard for humanity is perfection. Most of us readily admit that we don't know anyone who is perfect as God is perfect. The Bible shows the glory of God as our standard. Our sins stand in contrast to His glory, showing that we stand in need of His redemption. In Romans 3 Paul establishes the fact that God judges, regardless of a person's lifestyle or personal religion. He tells us that "there is no one who does good, there is not even one" (Rom. 3:12). All people have sinned and do not reflect God's righteousness and perfection.

A good way to help a person grasp that "all have sinned" is to turn to Matthew 22:37: "Love the Lord your God with all your heart, with all your soul, and with all your mind." You can ask, "Have you ever loved God with all your heart, soul, mind, and strength?" They will say no. Respond, "That's what sin is." This truth will make the word *sin*, which you highlighted in Romans 6:23, have a greater impact on the understanding of the person to whom you are witnessing.

Verse 2: Romans 6:23

Ask the person to read Romans 6:23 aloud: "The wages of sin is death, but the gift of God is eternal life in Christ Jesus our Lord." After he has finished, ask, "What does this verse say to you?"

Write your own response to this question.

Long + short-term outcome

It says that death is my paycheck for any sin I commit — but that if I am (in) Jesus, the paycheck becomes eternal life: Jesus flips the script! New outcome.

Sin

(and everyones)

Point out the word *sin*. Say something like "Did you notice that in my Bible I've underlined the word *sin*?" Point out that the word is *sin*, not *sins*. Give the person an opportunity to respond. Tell the person, "This reminds me that there is no *s* at the end of the word. God says that even one sin destines me for hell." Point to yourself so that you don't come across as holding yourself above being a sinner.

Point to the word *in* (or *through*, depending on the translation you are using), which you have circled. Point out that you have circled this word to remind you that becoming a Christian means you have a relationship with Jesus Christ. Many lost people place their hope for salvation in actions they may have done, such as baptism or church membership.

Roman 6:23 allows the Holy Spirit to show lost people that they have no hope without faith in Jesus. God's Word will have exposed false reasons for hope. The Holy Spirit will make the lost person understand a lot more from a simple reading of the verse than you can say. There are a lot of ways to share your faith, but Scripture introduces a different dynamic. You will be surprised how quickly some lost people become convinced of their need to trust Jesus as Savior and Lord. Watch God work as you guide a lost person to read the verses.

> ## There are a lot of ways to share your faith, but Scripture introduces a different dynamic.

I was asked to counsel a young woman who was in deep trouble. After asking her the five questions in the first step, it was apparent that she knew little about the Bible or Christianity. No one had ever shared Jesus with her. She gave me permission to open my Bible. She read Romans 3:23 aloud and told me what it said to her. I turned to Romans 6:23 and asked her to read it aloud. She spoke the verse slowly and clearly: "The wages of sin is death, but the gift of God is eternal life in Christ Jesus our Lord." I said, "What does that verse say to you?"

She thoughtfully replied, "I need to ask God to forgive me for all my sins and invite Jesus Christ into my heart." I was surprised. Does that verse say that? Not exactly. Where did she get her answer? The Holy Spirit.

I did not say, "Hold it; I have five more verses." Using the power of Scripture, God may reveal truth in one verse or in several verses. Your role is to simply turn the pages and ask questions.

Did he skip to invitation?

Never be afraid to witness to anyone. Although their experience, defenses, objections, and preconceived notions will play a role in their decision, the Holy Spirit is more powerful and the love of God is greater than anything that can darken the heart.

Verse 3: John 3:3

Ask the person to read John 3:3 aloud: "Unless someone is born again, he cannot see the kingdom of God." Remember, the X you drew reminds you that this Scripture is the exception to using the question "What does this verse say to you?" Instead, point to the cross you have drawn near the verse and ask, "Why did Jesus come to die?"

Write your own response to the question "Why did Jesus come to die?"

In this life, sin condemns me. I can't escape sin + death — I'm too weak. I need a 2nd chance, a new nature — but first Jesus clears the account + makes a diff. deposit

Most people will respond, "He came to die for sin." Respond, "That's right. Remember the verse you just read—the payment of sin is death." *His own righteous-ness*

> ## "Unless someone is born again, he cannot see the kingdom of God."
>
> JOHN 3:3

Verse 4: John 14:6

Turn to John 14:6 and ask the person to read this verse aloud: "I am the way, the truth, and the life. No one comes to the Father except through Me." Then ask, "What does this verse say to you?"

Write your own response to this question.

There is one way to God — Jesus is that way. Jesus brings the truth → enlightens us. Jesus reverses the death sentence → Jesus brings us to Life.

"I am the way, the truth, and the life. No one comes to the Father except through Me."

JOHN 14:6

The lost person will probably tell you that there is no other way to be with God except through Jesus. Because the verse is clear, you never have to add to it for the person to get its message.

A lost person may ask about other ways people can get to heaven. You don't have to refute those positions. John 14:6 will stick in the person's mind. Sharing Jesus in conversation with a lost person is always most effective when the witnessing Christian doesn't attempt to explain or discredit the false teachings and ideas that permeate our society. The key to sharing Jesus without fear is to present what the Bible says and let it stand on its own.

Verse 5: Romans 10:9-11

Ask the person to read Romans 10:9-11 aloud: "If you confess with your mouth, 'Jesus is Lord,' and believe in your heart that God raised Him from the dead, you will be saved. With the heart one believes, resulting in righteousness, and with the mouth one confesses, resulting in salvation. Now the Scripture says, 'No one who believes on Him will be put to shame.' " Then ask, "What do these verses say to you?"

Write your own response to this question.

Each of us must do more than "think" they believe Jesus is Lord' + was raised from death, We have to speak that this is truth.

One of the most difficult things for many people to believe is that they can be forgiven. You may not know the lost person's sins, but you can be sure that most lost people will think about particular sins. Any of a multitude of sins may come to mind—adultery, alcoholism, hatred, bitterness, or lies. If you do your part to lead the person to read God's Word, you can be sure God will convict them of their sins and pour out His power.

What if the person asks whether God will forgive those who have committed murder and other heinous sins? Let the Bible speak. Ask the person to read Romans 10:9-11 again. Trust the Holy Spirit to teach this person the truth of God's forgiveness.

Your objective is for the lost person to answer with a definite yes to the question "Does this truth in Romans 10:9-11 include me?" The Holy Spirit will be at work in the person's heart to help him or her understand God's unconditional love.

Avoid argument or defensiveness when the lost person doesn't understand. Apply what I call the read-it-again principle after any verses she doesn't understand. If someone does not understand or misunderstands a verse of Scripture, ask her in a loving way to read it again. God has been defending His Word for centuries. The Holy Spirit will guide the person to the truth. There is something wonderful about the way God opens the heart to understanding when a person reads the Bible aloud. God Himself is the witness to the truth you share.

Verse 6: 2 Corinthians 5:15

Ask the person to read 2 Corinthians 5:15 aloud: "He died for all so that those who live should no longer live for themselves, but for the One who died for them and was raised." After he has finished, ask, "What does this verse say to you?"

Write your own response to this question.

> "He died for all so that those who live should
> no longer live for themselves, but for the One
> who died for them and was raised."
>
> 2 CORINTHIANS 5:15

The lost person must understand that salvation—promised through Jesus' death—comes to all who surrender their lives to Him in faith. We are all on level ground at the cross. When we surrender to Christ as Savior, we are inwardly transformed to have new life. We are no longer slaves to sin and selfish desires. We have hearts turned to Jesus and His example for the way we should live. The Christian heart is freed by the power of the Holy Spirit from being self-centered to Christ-centered, which fills us with care for others.

Verse 7: Revelation 3:20

Ask the person to read Revelation 3:20 aloud: "Listen! I stand at the door and knock. If anyone hears My voice and opens the door, I will come in to him and have dinner with him, and he with Me." After he has finished, ask, "What does this say to you?"

Write your own response to this question.

The Lord Jesus knocks politely. He is not aggressive or a house breaker. We open the door, after we hear His voice, + become acquainted more + more.

"Listen! I stand at the door and knock. If anyone hears My voice and opens the door, I will come in to him and have dinner with him, and he with Me."

REVELATION 3:20

You want the lost person to understand that opening his heart to Jesus is his choice. Jesus is eager to come into our lives but never forces open the door.

Let's use this verse to learn more about applying the read-it-again principle. I have asked people to read Revelation 3:20 aloud and then to tell me what it says to them, only to hear a mistaken interpretation. A common misinterpretation is "Jesus will open the door and come into a person's heart." But the verse doesn't say Jesus will open the door. Each individual must open the door, and Jesus will come in. Jesus will not force His way into a person's heart. He will not come into a life uninvited. The best response when you recognize that the person doesn't understand is simply to say, "Read it again." You are not correcting or rescuing him. You are simply letting the Holy Spirit work.

Review the previous directions step by step, imagining how you would lead a lost person through the Scripture verses.

CLOSE WITH KEY QUESTIONS

Today you will learn how to approach the decision-making time in a witnessing encounter. Witnessing to a person does not depend on what you know but on the Person you know. That is an essential truth to keep in mind in order to share Jesus without fear. You are working in partnership with Almighty God. All the power of heaven will be unleashed for this moment when a lost person considers trusting Jesus and surrendering his or her life to Him. The gospel is simple. It is so simple that children can understand it. There is no reason an adult cannot understand and share it.

> ## Witnessing to a person does not depend on what you know but on the Person you know.

Remember, the five opening questions are designed to help you discover the person's spiritual condition and to open an opportunity to introduce the person to the truth of Scripture. Many lost people will receive the promises of Scripture if someone will use the Bible to tell them how. Some people will come under conviction before you have completed all the steps. When a person indicates that he or she is ready to make a commitment to Christ, it is best to proceed with the questions that guide him or her to do so.

Five closing questions provide a way for you to lead others to place their faith in Christ. Each question relates to one of the verses the lost person has read aloud. Through God's Word the Holy Spirit will have used Scripture to prepare the heart of the person to consider these questions.

1. **Are you a sinner?** People who have read the Scriptures and opened their hearts will say yes.

2. **Do you want forgiveness for your sins?** The Holy Spirit will have prepared the person's heart to understand that receiving forgiveness is his or her free choice.

3. **Do you believe Jesus died on the cross for you and rose again?** The person must understand that he or she must put his trust in Christ to be spiritually reborn.

4. **Are you willing to surrender your life to Christ?** The person will be open to the truth that the only way to be in a right relationship with God is through faith in Jesus Christ as Savior and Lord.

5. **Are you ready to invite Jesus into your life and into your heart?** If the person is ready, the Holy Spirit will use Revelation 3:20 to encourage him or her to open the door of his heart and surrender to Jesus.

Not "Is this the only way?" But "Why not take this way?"

Find these questions printed on the card you removed from the back of this book in week 2.

When you learn to ask these questions in a comfortable way, you will see what the Holy Spirit can do when a heart has been warmed by God's love. The Holy Spirit will have had an opportunity to touch the heart of the lost person. You haven't argued with or pressured the person. You will have been a kind, thoughtful listener to his thoughts about spiritual things. You will have shown him that you have great love and concern for him. You will be amazed by the simplicity of this approach, and you will rejoice to see God work.

After you ask the last question, "Are you ready to invite Jesus into your life and into your heart?" be silent and pray, allowing the Holy Spirit to work in the person's heart. Give the person time to say whatever he wants to say, praying silently as you listen.

Can you recall from week 1 the Holy Spirit's role in leading a lost person to Christ? Describe it here.

It is ALL the work of the Holy Spirit. I am not responsible for the outcome, just for the obedience to make the effort, to show a person who is open the Word.

You have just asked the person the most important question he will ever be asked in his life, and he will battle with Satan over who will control his life. You don't know whether he will live long enough to have another opportunity to accept Jesus. Take that possibility seriously. All the power of heaven is at work. Don't get in the way. Be silent and pray, letting the Holy Spirit do His work of convincing the person of his need for salvation in Jesus. That is His promise. You can trust Him to keep His word.

All the power of heaven is at work. Don't get in the way.

Two answers are possible when you ask, "Are you ready to invite Jesus into your life and into your heart?"—yes or no. Often a lost person will break the silence with a simple yes or "I'm ready." Ask, "What do you want to do?" Kindly guide him to state specifically that he wants to invite Jesus into his life.

Once the person has indicated that he wants to invite Jesus into his life, offer to lead him in a prayer of repentance and faith. The following prayer shows the elements to include. Notice that the content of the prayer responds to the five closing questions.

Heavenly Father, I have sinned against You.
I want forgiveness of all my sins. I believe
Jesus died on the cross for me and rose again.
Father, I give You my life to do with
as You wish. I want Jesus Christ to
come into my life and into my heart.
I ask this in Jesus' name.
Amen.

You must not assume that a lost person understands the meaning of praying a salvation prayer, signing a card, or walking down an aisle during an invitation in a worship service. Make sure the person understands that it is not these actions that save him but his decision to trust Jesus as Savior and Lord.

Don't neglect someone who has made a decision for Christ. Encourage them to grow as a disciple and to attend church. You might say something like this: "Now that you are a believer, God wants you to be involved in a fellowship of Christians. I'd like to help you get started." If she lives near your church, invite the person to go with you to your church. If not, you might say: "Do you think you would be more interested in a larger or smaller church?" After they respond, offer to help locate someone who will call within a few days.

Identify do's and don'ts to follow when leading someone to a decision for Christ. Write the appropriate word— do or don't—before each statement.

_____DO_____ be quiet and pray after asking question 5.

_____?___T__ intervene if, after asking question 5, the person *Ask why? AND Listen* seems to be struggling with a decision.

___DON'T___ indicate that a special prayer or joining a church will bring salvation.

_____DO_____ make it clear that a salvation prayer has no special saving power.

_____DO_____ invite a new believer to attend church with you. *or help connect them*

___DON'T___ consider your job done when the person has accepted Christ.

ANSWER THE NO RESPONSE WITH "WHY?"

How do you deal with the no response? A negative response is often expressed as "I'm not ready yet." The best response from you is to ask, "Why?" Then listen and use your spiritual thermometer. Let the answer reveal what is going on deep inside the person. Don't guess. Let him or her tell you.

There are many reasons a person may say he is not ready to trust Christ. The real reasons are usually far deeper than what is said, and only God knows what they are. Don't spend much time, if any, trying to clarify the reasons given. Keep the focus on the person's need to make a decision for Christ at that moment.

It is important to ask why a person has decided to reject Christ. You don't know whether it is something he has studied thoroughly, something he has heard, something he learned from his family as a child, or a bad experience in a church. The simple question "Why?" provides an opportunity to deal with the issue. You may find that an argument suddenly becomes small when the Holy Spirit works on it in love during a witnessing conversation.

Sometimes a person's response is "There are too many hypocrites in the church." Do you see what has happened? The person has switched from a hesitancy to accept Christ to a concern for hypocrites in the church. Respond with interest, saying something like "You know, I have thought about that a lot. I am sad to say that there are some disappointing people in churches. But I have great comfort in the Bible's teaching that we are to follow Jesus, not people. I've never found a perfect church, and I've come to realize that if I joined such a church, it would no longer be perfect. You could do a great service in a church because you are so sensitive to the harm done by hypocritical Christians." Using lighthearted tenderness will show that we can accept our weaknesses as Christians but that faith in Christ is paramount. This approach lets the person know that you aren't going to argue or become defensive. The battle is theirs, not yours.

Sometimes you will witness to bold individuals who will tell you that they live a sinful life and enjoy it. They may talk about the details of their sinful lifestyle with expressions of pride. I guide them to consider Jesus by saying, "I understand that you are not ready to change your life yet. But I want to make sure I have clearly shared the gospel with you. I have one more question. Let's imagine that tonight, since you have rejected Christ, you take part in some of the fun things you've talked about. Suppose that you are driving to one of the places you enjoy going to, and you are in an accident that takes your life. According to what you've read in the Bible [it is always wise to refer them to the authority of the Bible], because you died after deciding not to trust your life to Jesus, <u>what will happen to you?</u>" An acknowledgment of "Hell" is the usual response. My reaction is to say, "Forever is an awfully long time to spend in hell. But I hope you have a nice day." If the person doesn't decide to trust Jesus for his salvation, at least he will probably drive more carefully for a while.

"I'm not good enough" is a frequent response from persons who say no. Whatever the reasons are for not feeling good enough, remember the importance of taking the person to Scripture. A wonderful help is Romans 10:13: "Everyone who calls on the name of the Lord will be saved." I ask the person to read Romans 10:13 aloud. Sometimes I point out a terrible sin such as murder or something that may be a part of his own life, such as hatred or divorce. I say, "If a person is a murderer, a thief, or something like that, do you think that verse includes him?" Most people say yes. I respond, "Then can He forgive you?"

Rom 10:13

You may know the person well enough to know the source of his guilt. You could ask, "Do you think the verse [Rom. 10:13] includes people who have experienced situations similar to yours?" Help him understand that the greatest sin is to reject forgiveness and a relationship with Jesus as Savior and Lord. Ask the person to read aloud 1 John 1:7.

"If we walk in the light as He Himself is in the light, we have fellowship with one another, and the blood of Jesus His Son cleanses us from all sin."

1 John 1:7

1 JOHN 1:7

Then ask a question like "What does this verse say to you? What sin is not included in this statement? How many sins does the blood of Jesus purify?" Every person I've asked has replied, "All sins." You can then return to your last closing question: "Are you ready to invite Jesus into your heart and into your life?"

Another response given by persons rejecting Christ is "There are many religions in the world, and I don't know how a person can determine which one is right." I reply, "I have discovered that all of the religions in the world can basically be divided into two kinds. There are those that I will group by calling them the 'isms': Judaism, Mormonism, Buddhism, Hinduism, and others like them. All of these make two claims: (1) Jesus is not God, or He is not the only God. He may be a great prophet, a wise teacher, or a good man but not the Messiah. (2) If you do enough good works through your own efforts, you can receive some form of salvation.

"On the other hand, Christianity claims that Jesus is God and that God has come to us in Jesus, who lived, died on the cross, and rose from the grave so that we could have eternal life. Christianity claims, 'By grace you are saved through faith, and this is not from yourselves; it is God's gift—not from works, so that no one can boast' [Eph. 2:8-9]. Both of these teachings can't be true." Point out that every person must decide to place our trust in one view of Jesus or the other. This approach turns what may have been perceived as a huge, complicated argument into one that has a simple answer.

Briefly summarize an approach you could take to respond to each of the following objections.

1) **"I'm not ready yet."** Why? [Listen]

2) I understand what you say. But I have one more question. No one can know when they might die. After what we've read; what will happen if you died?

"There are too many hypocrites in the church."

Well, I understand what you say. Inside + outside of churches, you can run into people at all stages → getting free of sin — some slip here + there. Some disappoint us. But since we're all sinners saved by grace there is no perfect church... and yet I have always found the best fellowship there.

[left margin, handwritten, bottom to top] And our LORD never intended us to walk alone. BTW: we didn't go to church to do things; "We go there to thank God + give him praise." with others who have the same relationship?

2) **"I enjoy my sinful life."**

"I'm not good enough." Rom 10:13 Everyone who calls upon the name of the Lord will be saved.

b) It is a gift.

"There are many religions in the world, and I don't know
how a person can determine which one is right."

From what I can tell all of them fit into two camps 1) those that say Jesus isn't God or isn't the only God 2) those that require you to do "enough" (always unspecified) good works for some kind of salvation

Examine "36 Responses to Objections" on pages 98–108. Take Christianity does
note of ideas you can use when you encounter objections. neither.

If the person continues to say no, always remember that success as a witnessing Christian is not about you. It is about God and about your willingness to trust that you "do all things through Him who strengthens me" (Phil. 4:13). Our tendency is to read Paul's statement, "I can do all things," and then take inventory of our own strength, abilities, training, and situation. We observe our weaknesses and begin to list exceptions to "all things." The key is to remember the phrase "through Him." Paul's confidence was based on God's power, which worked through him.

That is the same promise God makes to you and me. God asks you to allow Him to work through you. The question is, Will you give Him the privilege of the process? Paul shared his faith "in weakness, in fear, and in much trembling" (1 Cor. 2:3). Paul made a difference, however, because he obeyed God, and God used him. God enabled him with the Holy Spirit. That same gift is yours as you share the good news.

4

LISTEN TO THE CONCERNS OF THE HEART

Rob had always been confident and satisfied with his non-Christian lifestyle. But one day a friend asked him a simple question: "Do you ever feel uncertain about what you are depending on spiritually for hope in your life?" That simple question unlocked a heart that had never allowed anyone in. Rob had never talked about how he really felt about spiritual things. But with help from his friend, Rob gave his heart to Christ. Today he believes that any life, no matter how tangled or distressed, can be set free if only someone cares enough to share.

Do you know a Rob, someone who is satisfied with their lostness? Write their name here and begin praying for an opportunity to share your faith. The Albrecht family
Joshua Pickett

The healing of a tangled, lost heart begins by helping the person turn that heart to consider Jesus. Resist the temptation to become involved in questions that don't involve the real issues of the lost person's heart. The more quickly you focus on Jesus' love and sacrifice, the more quickly faith will replace the confusion. A lost heart won't mind if your voice trembles or if you stumble over your words, betraying your lack of confidence in sharing Jesus. He or she will know by the power of the Holy Spirit and through your heartfelt concern that God's love is available.

A lost heart won't mind if your voice trembles or if you stumble over your words, betraying your lack of confidence in sharing Jesus.

Jesus was crucified between two criminals who were also crucified. One of these men, recognizing that Jesus was the Savior, pleaded, "Jesus, remember me when You come into Your kingdom!" (Luke 23:42). This criminal hadn't come to a clear understanding of his sin. He hadn't developed a sophisticated view of God. He didn't have the time or experience to learn what God is like. That wasn't the center of his concern. The Holy Spirit was at work. The man knew that this Jesus was God and that he had no hope unless Jesus responded to his plea, "Jesus, remember me."

This biblical account of a lost man's surrendering his life to Jesus reveals that a person doesn't need to know anything beyond a personal experience of Jesus' love. This criminal faced Jesus in person hanging on the cross. The Holy Spirit was working in the man's heart, and the man responded in faith. As you share Jesus in the best way you know how, that same power will be at work in the heart of the lost person. You cannot fail if you are obedient to witness. The decision of the lost person is based on her own freedom to choose as the Holy Spirit works in her life.

A person doesn't need to know anything beyond a personal experience of Jesus' love.

Many lost people have mistaken ideas about Christianity. As you witness to lost people, do not dwell on these issues; but be sensitive to the concerns of her heart. By showing patience and an ability to address their concerns, you will set a tone of honesty, compassion, and openness for the witnessing encounter. Here are some concerns you may hear.

"Being a Christian means keeping the Ten Commandments. Therefore, I must try harder to measure up." A young woman frequently came to a pastor in her community to ask for his prayers. She wanted to become a Christian. After his attempts to guide her in accepting Jesus as Savior and Lord, she always said, "Please keep praying for me that I will become a Christian. I'm trying." Finally, after one of her appeals for his prayers, the pastor kindly said to her, "You need to stop trying." Surprised, she said, "Surely you don't mean that." He replied, "Yes. I have always told you that I would pray for you as you continued trying to become a Christian. That was a mistake. Stop trying. Start trusting."

> "By grace you are saved through faith,
> and this is not from yourselves; it is God's gift—
> not from works, so that no one can boast.
> For we are His creation—created in Christ Jesus
> for good works, which God prepared ahead
> of time so that we should walk in them."
>
> EPHESIANS 2:8-10

We live in a culture that places great emphasis on doing, earning, and achieving. But Paul wrote in Ephesians 2:8-10, "By grace you are saved through faith, and this is not from yourselves; it is God's gift—not from works, so that no one can boast. For we are His creation—created in Christ Jesus for good works, which God prepared ahead of time so that we should walk in them." Christianity isn't a religion merely to teach people right and wrong; it's a relationship with Jesus Christ.

> Christianity isn't a religion merely to teach
> people right and wrong; it's a relationship
> with Jesus Christ.

A lost person needs help to understand that religious activity is a response to God because of the relationship rather than a way to achieve the relationship. Living a Christian life is a daily partnership with the living Lord. Lost people often have an impression that a person becomes a Christian by knowing certain facts and doing certain activities to maintain his status. He must understand that the Christian life begins as a decision in faith. Maturity develops as a person becomes more like Jesus through a daily relationship with Him.

"Becoming a Christian means giving up everything I enjoy." This is a partial truth. Some new Christians will need help to break their dependency on friendships and places that provide bad influences and on habits that encourage sinful actions. Those who truly seek God will find that He gives blessings that surpass the pleasures they have previously known.

Read John 16:20-24. What quality does Jesus' presence bring to our lives? *Peace. Joy.*

The joy that comes through a relationship with Jesus through faith is true joy. It is a gift of God, and it is not temporary. This joy is greater than the circumstances of our lives. Even in sacrifice—in giving up what we know is wrong—we have a joy that is not extinguished. The joy in a Christian's heart cannot be given or taken away by circumstances in our lives.

"God helps those who help themselves." This widely accepted statement, erroneously attributed to the Bible, is held by 56 percent of adults in America, according to a study done in 1990. The lost person holding this view approaches sin and salvation in either hopelessness or a sense of arrogance. Studies indicate that most societies around the world believe that everyone will ultimately receive reward and retribution according to what he deserves—how he has helped himself. This idea lies in the hearts of most lost people. For some, it provides a sense of hopelessness and despair as they are overwhelmed by the inability to rise above their sins. For others, it provides a false sense of security, arrogantly believing they can work to achieve salvation by their own merit.

Either: Life is hell + suffering or "Religion" is a crutch.

Even a casual reading of the Ten Commandments helps us realize that we can never keep all the demands of the law. The gospel of God's love and grace means that we don't have to. Paul wrote, "All who rely on the works of the law are under a curse, because it is written: 'Cursed is everyone who does not continue doing everything written in the book of the law.' Now it is clear that no one is justified before God by the law, because 'the righteous will live by faith.' But the law is not based on faith; instead, 'the one who does these things will live by them.' Christ has redeemed us from the curse of the law by becoming a curse for us. … The purpose was that the blessing of Abraham would come to the Gentiles in Christ Jesus, so that we could receive the promise of the Spirit through faith" (Gal. 3:10-14).

To the Ephesians Paul wrote, "God, who is abundant in mercy, because of His great love that He had for us, made us alive with the Messiah even though we were dead in trespasses. By grace you are saved!" (Eph. 2:4-5).

This is love without limits. God's wonderful love accepts us as we are and helps us become what we should be. We must represent God's true love to unbelievers. Sharing Jesus is not ignoring the reality of sin. A lost person must recognize, confess, and repent of his sins. But our witness is primarily of what Jesus has done in love for the sins of us all.

> ## Sharing Jesus is not ignoring the reality of sin. But our witness is primarily of what Jesus has done in love for the sins of us all.

Match each misconception about being a Christian with a Scripture that offers God's truth.

_B_ 1. "Being a Christian means keeping the Ten Commandments. Therefore, I must try harder to measure up."

    a. John 16:20-24

_A_ 2. "Becoming a Christian means giving up everything I enjoy."

    b. Ephesians 2:4-5

_C_ 3. "God helps those who help themselves."

    c. Ephesians 2:8-10

no one can boast of their works

SHARE YOUR HEART

Sharing Jesus is a means of opening your heart and lighting the undeniable truths of the Bible. God's Word is not merely an opinion. You present your beliefs through Bible verses that provide unchanging answers to the questions you ask.

Sharing your faith means creating an atmosphere of trust with a lost person. This trust allows a lost person to risk opening his heart about spiritual questions. The answers you provide are found in the Bible. These verses are the foundation for the spiritual peace, hope, and courage you have found for facing life's difficulties and complexities.

Many Christians state that while they were lost without Christ, they had a deep yearning to talk with someone about their spiritual needs. They speak of their fear of letting someone know their doubts and lack of knowledge. Many lost people want to understand more about the Bible but are unclear about what it actually says about Christ and salvation. God creates in the heart of every person the need to know the truth about Him.

The French philosopher Alexis de Tocqueville identified the moral attitudes of America's people as the source of their success. He referred to these beliefs that determine right and wrong and govern how we treat one another as habits of the heart. They are the heartfelt convictions that shape a person's actions and way of living.

Think about the seven Scriptures you will use to share your faith in Christ. What do they indicate are a believer's habits of the heart?

R 1) we see ourselves as sinners

R 2) we earn death, God gives us life (in) Jesus

J 3) I need a ♡ change + a rebirth to ever escape this + so learn

J 4) Jesus is (THE) only way → pays my debt
→ imputes His work to my acct

R 5) Begins c/ Belief + Speaking   6) We turn to the Lord + He takes it
                                          from here

7) We open
   the door

A believer's convictions are built on basic biblical teachings that provide assurance of the forgiveness of sins, the hope of eternal life, and the comfort of God's presence and care as we face life. The verses that provide the answers to the questions you ask a lost person are <u>not vague</u>. They are <u>not tools for manipulation</u>. They are the rock on which we stand as believers.

People have a lot of confusion about spiritual things. Disbelieving what the Bible says about Jesus is rarely the source of lost people's reluctance to talk about salvation. They are usually resistant because of an expectation that they will be critically judged, pressured, or sold. Asking pertinent, caring questions is the key. Your concern and willingness to listen quietly will be a great encouragement.

> Disbelieving what the Bible says about Jesus is rarely the source of lost people's reluctance to talk about salvation. They are usually resistant because of an expectation that they will be critically judged, pressured, or sold.

The apostle Paul wrote to young Timothy, "Have nothing to do with irreverent and silly myths. Rather, train yourself in godliness" (1 Tim. 4:7). In the same spirit, it is wise to discipline yourself for the purpose of sharing Jesus. Discipline yourself to listen with empathy. Listening to understand rather than to have an opportunity to speak is essential in gaining someone's trust. Listening with empathy shows that you want to understand and identify with the lost person.

To evaluate your listening skills, check the statements that are true of you. When someone talks about her thoughts, opinions, and feelings— *Depends on how I'm approached. The time...*

- ☑ **I mostly think about what I will say next;**
- ❑ **I listen with concentration and empathy;**
- ☑ **I listen selectively, paying attention only to what interests me;**
- ❑ **I get bored and tune out because I don't care.**
- ❑ **I try to focus on the other person's needs.**

If your listening habits reveal a lack of compassion and concern, begin praying that God will give you a heart that devotes time and attention to others.

A person replying to your questions will generally be trying to share feelings more than concrete facts that can be easily described. Listening helps you visualize in your mind how he feels about spiritual things. He must know that you understand and appreciate his views and feelings.

If given a chance, most people are open to opportunities to talk about their spiritual needs. A man said to me, "Sometimes I think it is useless to work and try to get ahead. I just seem to be getting nowhere." I responded with, "You know, I've felt that same way before. It's a feeling of hopelessness. What do you do when you feel this way? Do you have any kind of spiritual belief that gets you through?" He answered, "I don't guess I depend on anything but myself." A period of silence followed, and then he said, "I guess that shocks you, doesn't it?" I paused for a few seconds and said, "No, I can understand how you feel." I chose to leave it at that and asked question 2, "To you, who is Jesus?" I didn't attempt to explain why I could understand his feelings. But I sensed an immediate ease in our conversation from that moment until he prayed for Christ to forgive him and to come into his life.

[handwritten margin notes: Ask Q #1 / listen / receive the ans. c/ no or little comment]

God will open your eyes to wonderful witnessing opportunities when you have developed a heart for sharing Jesus through the process you have learned:

- Developing a passion for lost people *[handwritten: instead of apathy or fear]*
- Learning to lean on God's promises in prayer
- Taking steps to fulfill your partnership with God
- Trusting in the power of the Holy Spirit
- Preparing yourself to share Jesus

> God will open your eyes to wonderful witnessing opportunities when you have developed a heart for sharing Jesus.

Nevertheless, if you are not obedient to practice what you have learned, you will face one of two outcomes. First, you may lose heart and do nothing. Second, pride may grow in your heart for having learned how to share Christ.

Along with the process you have learned to witness, it is important to grasp the vision of Jesus' heartache for the lost.

Read John 4:4-42. How did Jesus' question to the woman at the well lead to a discussion of her spiritual need?

It was in the middle of the day and time to eat. Jesus put off eating to talk to a woman who had come to a well for water. He turned the conversation toward the deepest need of her heart by asking a simple question: "Will you give me a drink?" (John 4:7, NIV). Her reply opened the door for Jesus to talk about her spiritual emptiness. The power of the Holy Spirit continues to open hearts to Jesus' saving grace in that same way.

A simple question, "Do you have any kind of spiritual belief?" is often met with a response of openness because we are promised the power and partnership of the Holy Spirit as we obey the mandate to share our faith. When the disciples returned, they encouraged Jesus to eat: "The disciples kept urging Him, 'Rabbi, eat something' " (John 4:31). But He replied to His disciples' appeal, "I have food to eat that you don't know about" (John 4:32).

> "Listen to what I'm telling you:
> Open your eyes and look at the fields,
> for they are ready for harvest."
>
> JOHN 4:35

Jesus then appealed to His disciples, "Listen to what I'm telling you: Open your eyes and look at the fields, for they are ready for harvest" (John 4:35). They had spoken to Him about immediate hunger, but He knew they had not grasped the eternal consequences of their opportunity. The immediate physical satisfaction that would come from eating faded in importance as Jesus engaged in a greater satisfaction. The vision that drove Him was the prospect of a lost woman coming to trust Him for her salvation.

Keep your heart filled with the vision of joy and hope that enter the hearts of lost people who surrender in faith to Jesus.

Fill in the blanks to define what you have learned in this study about success in witnessing. Success in witnessing is not bringing someone to Christ but _living_ **the Christian life daily,** _sharing_ **the gospel, and** _trusting_ **God for the results.**

Success in witnessing is living the Christian life daily, sharing the gospel, and trusting God for the results. Success is not bringing someone to the Lord. We may share ineptly and with poor timing, but our Heavenly Father can use our faltering efforts if we have a heart to obey. The one thing He cannot use is our silence. He wants your obedience to the Great Commission.

All the work of evangelism is powered by the Word of God and the Holy Spirit. This is His job. We have the privilege of being part of the process. This is the Father's work from beginning to end. We must always look for where God is working and be attuned to the clues He gives us. We need to go through our daily lives in anticipation: "God, are You working here?"

God will bless you as you join Him in the exciting journey of sharing Jesus without fear. You will experience joy as you see our Lord drawing men, women, youth, boys, and girls to Himself and transforming their lives.

List the names of people with whom you plan to share Jesus.

Name   When

Read "My Personal Commitment with God to Share Jesus" on page 109. If this expresses your commitment, sign it with today's date.

Pray, thanking God for the things you have learned in this study. Recommit to sharing your faith with lost people. Ask for His heart to love them, His wisdom to discern their need, and His power to share Jesus without fear.

---

1. An inexpensive New Testament recommended for witnessing is *Share Jesus Without Fear New Testament*. See page 112 and the inside back cover of this book.

SMALL-GROUP EXPERIENCE | SESSION 4

Opening (15 minutes)

- Report on opportunities group members had to share their faith in the past week. If some have not shared their faith, be certain not to make them feel as if they have failed. Ask for the definition of *success*. Encourage members to be willing to share in the future.
- Think of one person you know (coworker, neighbor, business associate or client, family member) who you feel is the least likely to become a Christian.
  - **Option 1:** Draw a picture of that person.
  - **Option 2:** Write the initials of that person on the inside back cover of your workbook. List some characteristics of that person.
- What characteristics make us feel that some people are unlikely to receive Jesus as Savior and Lord?
- How does this perspective become a barrier to our sharing Jesus with certain people?

DVD (21:50 minutes)

- View the first DVD segment of Bill Fay's testimony, "A New Life." When the screen instructs you, stop.

Facilitator-Led Conversation (10 minutes)

- Why was Bill Fay an unlikely person to receive Jesus Christ as Savior and Lord?
- Did any of the people Bill Fay rejected really fail?
- Do you think God could use you to reach the person you thought about earlier in this session?

Review (8 minutes)

What has God taught you through *Share Jesus Without Fear?*

DVD (7:30 minutes)

- View the second DVD segment with William Fay's closing challenge, "A New Life: Part 2." When the screen instructs you, stop.

Closing (10 minutes)

- Read "My Personal Commitment with God to Share Jesus" on page 109 in the workbook and, if you are willing to make this commitment, sign it.
- Remember that success in witnessing is living the Christian life daily, sharing the gospel, and trusting God for the results. Success is not bringing someone to Christ.
- Pray for specific persons with whom you plan to share the gospel. Pray that God will give you courage and opportunities to share Jesus without fear.

36 RESPONSES TO OBJECTIONS

In my experiences in sharing the gospel, I have encountered individuals who expressed resistance. Here are some of the common objections I have heard after using the why principle. Use the accompanying responses to answer objections you may encounter when witnessing.

1. I'm not ready.

ASK: *Why?* Allow your friend to answer. *Are you really going to let not being ready stand between you and God?* If the answer is no, ask: *Are you ready to invite Christ into your life?*

Your friend may respond: *I'm not ready because this information is so new to me. This is a whole new way of thinking, and I want to count the cost.* Be prepared to stop the presentation and release your friend to God's sovereignty and control.

SAY: *I enjoyed our talk, and I will pray for you. May I talk to you again in a few days or weeks?*

2. My friends will think I'm crazy.

SAY: *If they are really your friends, won't they be happy and thrilled that the God of the universe lives inside you and that all of your sins are forgiven? After all, when they see you change, they may want what you have. "There is joy in the presence of God's angels over one sinner who repents"* (Luke 15:10). *Are you ready?*

3. What about my family?

ASK: *What about your family?* Have the person read aloud Matthew 10:37-38 and Luke 12:51-53. *What do these verses say to you?*

Are you ready to pray?

4. I've done too many bad things.

See objection 32, "I'm not good enough," or objection 31, "God cannot forgive me."

5. I'm having too much fun.

Repeat what your friend answers.

SAY: *In other words, you are into the party scene—sex, drugs, and rock and roll.*

ASK: *According to this, when you die, where are you going?* If he answers *hell*, ask: *Are you ready to accept Jesus Christ as your Savior?* If the answer is no, say: *Drive carefully* or *Have a nice day.*

You may need to release your friend from this conversation, but be sure to give him your phone number if he wants to call you back in a few days. Keep praying.

6. Why does God let bad things happen?

Your friend may be dealing with a tragedy. Allow him to vent if he wants. Your job is to listen. Respond when he is finished.

SAY: *You may wonder why God allowed that to happen to you. But here are your choices: you can walk through the rest of your life alone in your pain, or you can choose to hold on to a nail-scarred hand. What do you want to do?*

7. There are many paths to God.

Have the person read aloud John 14:6. Ask: *What does it say to you?* Have the person read aloud Philippians 2:9-11. Ask: *What does it say to you?*

SAY: *What are you going to say when you stand before God? He is going to meet you either as your Savior or as your Judge.*

ASK: *Are you ready to invite Christ into your heart?*

8. There are many religions in the world.

SAY: *I've discovered that all of the religions in the world can be divided into two groups. Imagine every religion other than Christianity is in my left hand—Mormonism, Buddhism, Hinduism, Judaism, Islam—and Christianity is in my right hand. Everyone in my left hand makes two distinctive claims: (1) Jesus is not God, or He is not the only God. He may be a great prophet, a wise teacher, or a good man; but He is not the Messiah. (2) If you do enough good works through your own efforts, such as terrorist acts, religious acts, or good deeds, you can receive salvation.*

Two opposite claims cannot possibly be true. I would be willing to admit that if the pile of religions in my left hand is true, my faith is in vain. Would you be willing to admit if Christianity, in my right hand, is true, that your faith is in vain? Let's examine the evidence so that we can find out which one of us is possibly in error.

Christianity claims that Jesus is God and that God has come to us in Jesus, who lived, died on the cross, and rose from the grave so that we could have eternal life. Christianity claims that you are saved by grace through faith and not by works.

Have the person read aloud Ephesians 2:8-9. Ask: *What does it say to you?* Have the person read aloud John 14:6. Ask: *What does it say to you? Many religions and many ways to God, or Jesus is the only way to God? Can both of these teachings be true?*

9. I've always believed in God.

Have the person read aloud James 2:19. Ask: *What does it say to you?*

SAY: *I'm glad you believe in God. That's wonderful. But so does the devil. In fact, he's even seen God. How are you any different? Would you like to receive Jesus as your Savior?*

10. There are too many hypocrites in the church.

SAY: *You are absolutely correct. There are hypocrites in every church. I'm so glad you are concerned about that, because when you join the perfect church, it won't be perfect any longer. Jesus said not to follow hypocrites but to follow Him. I'm glad you know the difference between a hypocrite and a genuine person.*

Smile. *If you accept Christ as your Savior, and I see you begin to act like a hypocrite, I will remind you of this conversation. Are you ready to pray?*

Some of your friends may want to discuss dishonest TV evangelists or others who misrepresent Christ. In this event say: *If I falsely represented myself to you as a realtor in order to scam your money, does that mean all realtors are dishonest? Of course not. Just because a person says he represents Christ does not mean he is a representative of Christ. Only Christ knows his heart. Would you let a dishonest person stand in the way of your knowing God's love for you? Are you ready to pray?*

11. I don't believe in God.

ASK: If this objection is stated at the end of the presentation, ask: *Why?*

If you became convinced that God exists, would you be willing to give your life to Him? Would you be willing to ask a nonexistent God to help you in your unbelief?

PRAY: *God, if You are real, help me believe.*

SAY: *Let's talk again in a few days or weeks.*

If further help is needed, recommend that your friend read *More than a Carpenter* by Josh McDowell.

12. I'm a member of another world religion.

ASK: *Has anyone ever told you about Christianity? Let me show you some Scriptures that help explain this idea.* Show the Share Jesus Scriptures.

13. I'm Jewish.

ASK: When someone says he doesn't believe in Jesus, ask: *Why not?* If he says he is Jewish, then ask: *Do you go to synagogue anywhere? Did you know that Judaism is the root of my faith in Christianity?*

SAY: *I believe Jesus is the Christ, the Messiah. Did you know He claimed to be God?* Have the person read aloud John 10:30. Ask: *What does it say to you?*

I know He is not a liar, because He never sinned. He's obviously not a lunatic, because His life and teachings show He was brilliant, stable, and loving toward others. Therefore, I can only believe He is Lord.

Also, the Jews of the day clearly knew who Jesus claimed to be, because they tried to kill Him. Have the person read aloud John 8:58. Ask: *What does it say to you? The Jewish people knew He was referring to Himself with the divine name of God found in Exodus 3:14.*

If Jesus is the Messiah and He rose from the dead, would you consider having a personal relationship with Him to complete your Jewishness?

Ask the person to read Isaiah 53 aloud. Ask: *What does it say to you?*

- *Whom do you think this describes?*
- *Why do you think many synagogues refuse to read this chapter of Isaiah?*
- *Do you know why the sacrifices have stopped in the temple?* After they answer, continue: *Could it be because Jesus is God's sacrificial lamb?*

Don't push. Your goal is to have a warm, friendly discussion that will lead to other discussions. If the person indicates an interest in learning more, invite him to meet with a local messianic pastor, who is more an expert on the Old Testament than you. A fellow Jew will be sensitive to your friend's

culture and feelings. Encourage your friend to visit a messianic congregation with you, where he can see Jewish people expressing their faith in Christ.

If you determine that your friend does not attend synagogue and is what I call a secular Jew, lead him through the same Scriptures about Christ found in objection 14, "Cults are the answer." You may also want to give him a copy of Josh McDowell's book *More than a Carpenter* or a copy of the Gospel of John to read.

14. Cults are the answer.

ASK: *If what you believe were not true, would you want to know? Who is Jesus Christ? Isn't it interesting He said He was God?*

Have the person read aloud the following verses. Ask: *What does it say to you?*

- John 10:30 (The literal translation means Jesus and the Father are of the same essence.)
- John 14:7
- Revelation 1:8
- Colossians 1:15-16
- John 8:58
- Exodus 3:14 (The Jewish people wanted to stone Jesus in John 8:58 because they knew He was referring to Himself as God when He called Himself I AM. He was using the divine name of God found in Ex. 3:14.)

- John 5:18
- John 20:28-29
- Hebrews 1:6 (Ask: *Did Jesus ever sin?*)
- Hebrews 4:15 (Ask: *Who can forgive sins but God alone? If Jesus was not God, how could He forgive sins and not sin Himself?*)
- Matthew 9:2-6 (Ask: *Why did Jesus allow others to worship Him if He was not God?*)
- John 9:38

SAY: *Jesus said He was God. If He was a good man and never sinned, then how could He lie? He also allowed others to worship Him and forgave sins. How could He do this if He was not God?*

Some unbelievers will not understand how God the Son and God the Father can be one and the same. In this case say: *I am a son and a brother* (or whatever pronouns best describe you). *Although I have two different roles, I am the same person. God is both God the Son and God the Father. He has different roles, but He is the same person. Would you like to know Him?*

ASK: *May I show you a few Scriptures that changed my life?* Show the Share Jesus Scriptures or ask: *May I tell you how Christ changed my life?*

15. How can a loving God send someone to hell?

ASK: *Why would God allow His Son, Jesus, to die on the cross for us if His death had no meaning?* Have the person read aloud Romans 8:32. Ask: *What does it say to you?* Have the person read aloud Romans 6:23. Ask: *What does it say to you?*

SAY: *Jesus died for us so that we would not have to go to hell.* Have the person read aloud Romans 5:8-9. Ask: *What does it say to you?*

If you reject Christ and His gift, what does Scripture say will happen to you?

Jesus died in our place. If this were not the case, don't you think God would have spared His own Son? He died in your place. Would you like to be forgiven through His sacrifice?

16. How can I know the Bible is true?

ASK: *How many people would it take to flip a quarter before one person hits heads 30 times in a row?* (One billion.) *One reason I believe the Bible is true is the 30 recorded prophecies of Jesus' birth, death, and resurrection that have come true. That's a lot like landing heads 30 times in a row.*

How many people would it take to flip a quarter before one person hit heads 245 times in a row? This is a conservative estimate of the number of biblical prophecies that have come true. Have the person read aloud 2 Peter 1:21. Ask: *What does it say to you?*

May I share some Scriptures that changed my life?

17. I don't believe the resurrection took place.

SAY: *I'm glad this is your only stumbling block, because God has provided overwhelming evidence of the resurrection. In fact, a mock trial was held at Harvard University, and the evidence overwhelmingly proved the resurrection of Jesus Christ.* Have the person read aloud Jeremiah 29:13. Ask: *What does it say to you?*

If you want to test your heart right now, why don't you bow your head?

PRAY: *Lord Jesus, if the resurrection took place, help me in my unbelief.*

If your friend is ready, you may have him pray: *I am a sinner. I want forgiveness of all my sins. I want to believe that Jesus died on the cross for my sin.*

ASK: *Did you mean this prayer? God will help you believe.*

If your friend wants to see Scripture that addresses the deity of Christ, see objection 14, "Cults are the answer."

18. You can't possibly know what truth is.

ASK: *What if I asked to borrow your watch, put it in my pocket, and refused to give it back? What would your reaction be?* He will probably say that he would insist that you return it, saying something like: *Hey, that's my watch! Give it back!*

Ask: *What if I refused, arguing that my truth is taking watches from people who don't believe in truth?* He will probably protest, saying that would be stealing. Ask: *Why is it wrong to steal?* He will probably say: *It just is.* Ask: *How do you know? You just told me there are no rights or wrongs. How can it be wrong if I steal your watch?*

SAY: *I'll tell you how I know it's wrong. Because God says so. You can't hide behind the statement that there is no truth. May I show you some verses of Scripture that have had a major impact on my life?*

19. There are many translations of the Bible.

This objection usually appears at the beginning of the Share Jesus presentation.

SAY: *You are correct. Did you know they all say the same thing? Let's turn to Romans 3:23.*

20. There are too many errors in the Bible.

Hand your friend your Bible and ask: *Would you show me one?* When he says he can't, say: *I can't either. Let's turn to Romans 3:23.*

21. What about those who never hear the gospel?

ASK: *That's not you, is it? What does the Bible say will happen to those who have heard and have not responded?* Have the person read aloud Romans 1:20. Ask: *What does it say to you?*

SAY: *Now you've heard the gospel. Will you respond?*

22. You must think you are better than I.

SAY: *I am not better than you; I am simply better off. Like you, I have broken God's commandments and laws and was condemned to hell. But by His grace and unfailing love, God sent someone into my life to tell me about Jesus. That made me realize how dirty I was in the presence of the holy God.*

I asked God to forgive me, and He did. It doesn't make me better than you; it makes me forgiven.

Now I am giving you the same opportunity someone gave me. Would you like to be forgiven and know what it is like to be born again and have a personal relationship with Jesus Christ?

23. I'm a good person.

ASK: *By whose standards? Have you ever committed murder?* After your friend's responses to the previous questions, continue with the following, but do not allow him to respond to the questions.

SAY: *Let's check it out by God's definition. Have you ever been angry or hated, called someone a fool, or waved them off on the freeway? Because if you have, by God's standards you are a murderer.*

Have you ever looked at the opposite sex and lusted? By the way, if you say no, I know you are lying. But if you have lusted, by God's standards you are guilty of adultery.

Have you put a relationship, a job, or an activity above a relationship with God? If you have, those items are your idols.

Because of God's holiness, it is impossible to measure up to His standards of perfection. Because God is the judge and the jury, it is His approval we have to meet.

Have the person read aloud James 2:10. Ask: *What does it say to you?*

I want you to know that I, like you, have been guilty as well. The difference is that I found forgiveness through Jesus. Do you want this kind of forgiveness?

Remember to be loving to your friend. God is still in control of his life.

24. I'm God.

SAY: *I could use a new car. Could you create one for me? Surely, an all-powerful God like you can do that.*

Have the person read aloud Exodus 20:3. Ask: *What does it say to you?* Have the person read aloud Romans 1:25. Ask: *What does it say to you?* Have the person read aloud Colossians 1:13-17. Ask: *What does it say to you?*

According to this Scripture, God is God alone. He is not "all things," but He is the Creator who holds all things together. I am not God, but He is in me. Would you like God to be in you?

25. I'm not a sinner.

Ask the person to read aloud Matthew 22:37. Ask: *What does it say to you? Have you ever loved God with all your heart, soul, mind, and strength? If not, that's what sin is. Let's turn to the next Scripture.*

26. A Christian hurt me.

SAY: *I'm so sorry that happened. Would you accept my apology for those who did that to you? Have you ever tried to love somebody* and made a mess out of it? You had good intentions, but everything went wrong. Do you think there was a possibility in your friend's desire for you to know Jesus that she just went about it the wrong way?*

Jesus would not approve of rude behavior either. By the way, what is your understanding of who Jesus is?

27. The church only wants my money.

ASK: *Has the church ever asked you for money? It's true that most churches take an offering. But it is usually the members who are expected to give, not the visitors.*

God doesn't want your money. But when you become a believer, something happens to your heart. You give because you want to. If you don't give from joy, you shouldn't give at all.

The church doesn't want your money; the church wants you to surrender your life to Jesus. Are you willing to do that?

28. I've tried it, and it didn't work out.

ASK: *What have you tried? If your friend says something like, I tried that prayer once, and nothing happened, say: Apparently, that's true. Did you mean the prayer when you said it?*

Usually, he's not 100 percent sure. *Tell me about the moment you gave your life to Christ.*

Does his testimony make sense? Does it sound true? *Let's take a minute and review the Scriptures. Read them aloud; then tell me what they mean.*

If his testimony does not sound true, say: *If you never found a desire to read your Bible or fellowship with other believers, there is a possibility you were never born again. Would you like to make sure?*

If he says yes, say: *Let's review the Scriptures to help you get a better understanding of the gospel.* Show him the seven Share Jesus Scriptures and lead him in prayer.

29. How do I know I have enough faith?

SAY: *If you have enough faith to ask Christ to come into your heart, you have enough faith to receive Him into your heart.*

Imagine Moses. As he led his people out of Egypt, he met a pretty big roadblock—the Red Sea. As Pharaoh's army closed in on Moses and the tribes of Israel, God directed Moses to cross the sea. Moses stood on the shore wondering whether he had enough faith. It wasn't until he put his foot in the water that the sea parted. God will also honor your first step.

If you really want to know Jesus as Lord, take the first step and ask Him into your heart. Are you ready?

30. I can't live the Christian lifestyle.

SAY: *I am glad you understand some change is required. But unlike in the past, you will not have to change alone.*

Ask the person to read aloud Philippians 4:13. Ask: *What does it say to you?*

God wants your "want to," not your ability. He wants your desire. Are you desiring now to follow Jesus Christ as your Lord? If your friend says yes, it is time for the salvation prayer.

31. God cannot forgive me.

Ask the person to read aloud Romans 10:13. Ask: *What does it say to you?*
ASK: *Can God forgive a repentant murderer? Can He forgive a bank robber? Can God forgive you?* If your friend answers yes, say: *Let's pray.*

32. I'm not good enough.

SAY: *That's one thing we have in common. We are not good enough. This is a problem. There are only two ways to get to heaven: either we have to be perfect, never once* committing a sin in word, deed, or thought, or we have to become born again. I can become born again by accepting in my heart the finished work and person of Jesus Christ, who paid the penalty for my sins. He has the power to forgive me because of His birth, death, and resurrection. When I believe in Him and accept His forgiveness, only then can He erase the sins I have committed in the past. Personally, I opt to choose His forgiveness, because I can never be good enough to attain perfection.

Have the person read aloud Ephesians 2:8-9. Ask: *What does it say to you?* Have the person read aloud Romans 10:9-10. Ask: *What does it say to you?* Have the person read aloud Romans 10:13. Ask: *What does it say to you? Does this include you? Are you ready for God to forgive your sins?*

I imagine that before you asked Christ into your life, you didn't go around worrying that Christ was not in your heart. Your concern is a wonderful confirmation to me that you might be saved.

Have the person read aloud Romans 8:38-39. Ask: *What does it say to you?* Have the person read aloud Ephesians 1:13-14. Ask: *What does it say to you?*

The moment you invited Christ into your life, you were saved. God guarantees that one day you will be with Him in heaven. Most Christians have experienced the fears you have. But you must move past these fears so that you can grow in your faith. You will find that reading your Bible, praying, and spending time with other believers will strengthen your faith. Let me help you get started. May I pick you up for church next Sunday?

33. I'm not sure I'm saved.

Sometimes you will meet someone who has genuinely asked Christ into his heart but feels that he is not saved.

SAY: *That's a very nice watch. If you lost it, you'd miss it when you wanted to see the time. But if you had never owned a watch, you wouldn't worry about looking at it, nor would you worry about losing it.*

Don't you find it interesting that you are worried you are not saved? You can't worry about losing something you don't have.

34. My beliefs are private.

ASK: *If what you believe were not true, would you want to know? May I share some Scriptures with you?*

You are trying to discover his real objection. Chances are, he has been hurt by a Christian in the past. If he describes a bad experience with a Christian who tried to witness to him, see objection 26, "A Christian hurt me."

35. I want to think about it.

Ask the person to read aloud Romans 6:23. Ask: *What does it say to you?*

ASK: *According to this, when you die, where are you going?* If your friend answers *hell*, ask: *Are you ready to accept Jesus Christ as your Savior?* If the answer is no, say: *Drive carefully* or *Have a nice day.*

If he says he is not ready, you will need to release him from this conversation, but be sure to give him your phone number in case he wants to call you in a few days. Keep praying. Also see objection 1, "I'm not ready."

36. The argument never stops.

ASK: *Why are you angry? Why does the presentation of the gospel make you hostile? If for some reason you found out that everything I've said about the gospel and about Jesus were true, what would you do about it?*

If he says he will not believe, ask: *Why?* Otherwise, say: *That's wonderful, because I was the same way.* You may want to give him a short testimony of how Jesus changed your life.

Try to get him to open up with one or more of the following questions: *I was open with you about my life. What was the most traumatic thing that has ever happened to you? Do you have a fear? Are you afraid of death? Did your parents ever hurt you? Would accepting God's love scare you to death? Has anyone ever loved you? Do you ever feel alone? Would you like to accept Jesus as your Savior?*

Do not feel like a failure if he does not respond. Keep praying for him.

MY PERSONAL COMMITMENT WITH GOD TO SHARE JESUS

I will no longer be a silent Christian.

I will continually look for those in whom You are working and for ways I can share Jesus with them.

Because I understand that Christ's resurrection power lives in me and that I lack nothing to keep my Lord's Great Commission, I will obey that command to go and make disciples.

I will live my life in a way that actively demonstrates Philemon 6, allowing You to fulfill Your promises in my life:

"I pray that you may be active in sharing your faith, so that you will have a full understanding of every good thing we have in Christ." PHILEMON 6, NIV

Signed _____ Date _____

Two Ways to Earn Credit
for Studying LifeWay Christian Resources Material

CHRISTIAN GROWTH STUDY PLAN

CONTACT INFORMATION:
Christian Growth Study Plan
One LifeWay Plaza, MSN 117
Nashville, TN 37234
CGSP info line 1-800-968-5519
www.lifeway.com/CGSP
To order resources 1-800-458-2772

Christian Growth Study Plan resources are available for course credit for personal growth and church leadership training.

Courses are designed as plans for personal spiritual growth and for training current and future church leaders. To receive credit, complete the book, material, or activity. Respond to the learning activities or attend group sessions, when applicable, and show your work to your pastor, staff member, or church leader. Then go to *www.lifeway.com/CGSP*, or call the toll-free number for instructions for receiving credit and your certificate of completion.

For information about studies in the Christian Growth Study Plan, refer to the current catalog online at the CGSP Web address. This program and certificate are free LifeWay services to you.

Need a CEU?

CONTACT INFORMATION:
CEU Coordinator
One LifeWay Plaza, MSN 150
Nashville, TN 37234
Info line 1-800-968-5519
www.lifeway.com/CEU

Receive Continuing Education Units (CEUs) when you complete group Bible studies by your favorite LifeWay authors.

Some studies are approved by the Association of Christian Schools International (ACSI) for CEU credits. Do you need to renew your Christian school teaching certificate? Gather a group of teachers or neighbors and complete one of the approved studies. Then go to *www.lifeway.com/CEU* to submit a request form or to find a list of ACSI-approved LifeWay studies and conferences. Book studies must be completed in a group setting. Online courses approved for ACSI credit are also noted on the course list. The administrative cost of each CEU certificate is only $10 per course.

LifeWay
Biblical Solutions for Life

Holman CSB
Share Jesus Without Fear
New Testament

HOLMAN
CHRISTIAN STANDARD BIBLE®

Share Jesus Without Fear New Testament takes you beyond the concerns of rejection and not knowing what to say and provides a progressive, step-by-step rationale that leads non-Christians into a realization of their current life choice. The lost are then afforded the opportunity to accept Christ. With its "Share Bible Directions" and powerful "Response Scripts to Objections," this New Testament can pack the kind of power that only the Holy Spirit can generate to encourage and strengthen new believers and old alike.

Convenient to carry and never intimidating, this comfort-trim New Testament is about the size of a checkbook, easily fitting into any purse, coat pocket, or shirt pocket. Ideally suited for sharing the gospel and leaving with the person. Inexpensively priced for mass distribution.

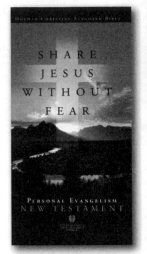

Format: Paperback
ISBN: 978-1-5864-0445-1
Case Quantity: 48
Case Price: $96.00

**Not Sold Individually
Case Orders Only**

Features include:

- Introduction and special notes by *Share Jesus Without Fear* author Bill Fay
- Words of Christ in red
- 36 answers for most common objections to receiving Christ
- Five-step witnessing plan with suggested Scriptures
- Presentation page

www.HolmanBibleOutreach.org
(866) 627-7796

Holman Bible Outreach International is a ministry created to facilitate the translation, production, and distribution of affordable Bibles and Scripture portions for evangelism, mission projects, training, and other forms of ministry.

HOLMAN
**BIBLE
OUTREACH**
INTERNATIONAL